Aᴬⁿ– Z₍ₒ𝒻₎
Finance

The Daily Telegraph

An A–Z of Finance

A Jargon-Free Guide to Investment and the City

MICHAEL BECKET

KOGAN PAGE

The masculine pronoun has been used throughout this book. This stems from a desire to avoid ugly or cumbersome language, and no discrimination, prejudice or bias is intended.

YOURS TO HAVE AND TO HOLD
BUT NOT TO COPY

First published in 1976
Second edition 1981
Third edition 1987
First published by Kogan Page in 1999

Kogan Page Limited
120 Pentonville Road
London N1 9JN

British Library Cataloguing in Publication Data

A CIP record for this book is available from the British Library.

ISBN 0 7494 2816 3

All illustrations by Hewison
Typeset by Kogan Page Ltd
Printed and bound by Clays Ltd, St Ives plc

A down-to-earth guide to the financial jargon of headlines: it explains ordinary shares and convertibles, what the International Monetary Fund does, and why currencies float. The book also provides an authoritative but entertaining explanation of monetarism and Green Pound, base rate, USM, what unemployment figures mean, and much more.

'Mr Becket does not just keep the language uncomplicated. He manages to inject a light touch and add some extra erudition... This book is actually fun to read.' **THE GUARDIAN**

'A bright easy style which even the most financially mind-blocked should be able to understand... You need to know about such things if you want to keep up with what's going in the world.' **SUNDAY TIMES**

'Highly recommended.' **THE DIRECTOR**

'Useful... it explains everything from accepting house to zollverein.' **THE DAILY TELEGRAPH**

'Enormously useful to people who teach economics or indeed anyone who does not know their assets from their elbow and wants to find out painlessly.' **THE GUARDIAN**

'Recommended for effortless reading.' **TOLLEY'S TAX GUIDE**

Who this book is for

Newspapers and broadcasters seem to assume everybody knows about money supply and eurocurrencies, can distinguish between the World Bank and the International Monetary Fund, and knows what EMU, OECD, FSA, ADR, etc stand for.

A layman needs a guide through the jungle of jargon and this book explains most of the commonly used terms in straightforward language that sometimes mocks the pomposity of the City.

We all need to understand what is happening in the world of finance, what the Chancellor of the Exchequer is up to, what the unions are attempting, and what the prospects are for the economy. Economists and journalists try to hide commonplace and inaccurate ideas behind a veil of complicated language – this book helps readers hack their way through to the real meaning.

It is for all ages and all walks of life, from the schoolchild who wants explanations of novel expressions, through shareholders coming to terms with the City, to the average citizen trying to follow the news.

AAA

The top rating for corporate securities – ie bonds issued by organizations (corporate and municipal) of unquestioned solidity – issued by Standard and Poor's, and Moody's, two US credit rating companies.

Accepting house

What it accepts is bills of exchange (qv) and so guarantees the company will be paid. Naturally, it charges for the service, but at least the bill can then be discounted at a good rate on the money market. As bills of exchange have faded from fashion, most houses have reverted to their original main function of merchant banking.

Accident insurance

See Health insurance.

Accrual rate

The rate at which money builds up in a scheme, such as a pension fund.

Accumulation units

Investors not interested in immediate income can opt to have dividend payments from a unit trust rolled up into capital value.

These are accumulation (as opposed to income) units and stand at a higher price.

Acid test

One of the rough measures purporting to measure the health of a company. If the cash and near-cash (readily saleable assets such as shares) are less than half current liabilities, the company may be overstretched and be in difficulties in emergencies.

Actively managed

The manager of an investment portfolio is actually trying to do well by beating the average. The plan is to produce a performance superior to the FT-SE 100 Index. For a contrary view, see Tracker.

Actuary

Snide people say an actuary is someone who likes maths but cannot stand the excitement of accountancy. In fact, they are specialist statisticians calculating the probabilities of people dying and the likely costs of insuring them. So they are largely responsible for setting the cost of life assurance and pension contributions.

Additional voluntary contributions

People worried that their company pension will not keep them in anything like a decent lifestyle after they retire, can pay into tax-efficient schemes which top up the pension.

The free-standing sort go into schemes operated by organizations like insurance companies and offer a wide range of investments. But the cost will be higher than putting more into the employer's own scheme.

Administration order

The Insolvency Act 1986 introduced a device which allows courts to issue an order protecting a precarious company from its enraged creditors who might want to put it into receivership or even liquidation. The aim is to give it time to restructure and present a plan that will allow it either to survive or at least to realize assets in a methodical fashion that will yield maximum returns.

ADR

See American Depositary Receipts.

After hours trading

The Stock Exchange is steadily dispensing with the enviably civilized hours dealers used to keep as it tries to keep up with world markets. Now trading starts at 8.30 in the morning and stops at 4.30 in the afternoon. But even then the demands of the Far East at one end of the day and the USA at the other means that stock market firms are working longer hours than that. Trading that takes place after the official closing hours will not appear in the closing price and will be reported to the exchange authorities the next day.

Allotment

Horticulture only in the sense that the plums of the investment world's new issues tend to be oversubscribed. If it is really popular, the issue can be oversubscribed ten times or more. In that case the big orders are usually scaled down and sometimes only the minimum applications get all they asked for. The amount the subscribers actually get is called the allotment and they get a letter notifying the basis well before the shares actually arrive.

Allotment letter

Letter from a company notifying applicants that they have been successful in getting shares when the company goes public.

Alternative investments

It was unnecessarily confusing or devious of the stock exchange to have renamed the cadet branch of the main listing as Alternative Investment Market because for a very long time the normal way of referring to investing money in something other than gilts or shares has been as alternative investments.

That is still how most newspapers refer putting money into stamps, 18th century English drinking glasses, old master drawings or classic cars. Most of these areas are traps for the layman who does not know the value of an individual item much less the trend of the market as a whole. Other problems are shortage of independent assessment of worth, no recognized continuous market which would also set prices, and a swarm of plausible conmen. Calling them investments is probably misleading as most of them are little more than a gamble.

Alternative Investment Market

A sort of half-way house quotation on the stock market for smaller and younger companies which would not be able to meet the full listing requirements. It replaced a previous such effort by the Stock Exchange to persuade businesses to overcome the pain and problems of public listing – the Unlisted Securities Market, which was similar but widely ignored and finally died of apathy.

American Depositary Receipts

If US investors want to buy shares not quoted in the United States, they often do so via a bank, such as Morgan Guaranty, which acquires the overseas stock, and then issues a sort of bearer bond acknowledging the owner's entitlement. These are called American Depositary Receipts, ADRs for short.

Amortization

US for depreciation.

Analyst

Stockbrokers employ clever young people who scrutinize the annual reports of companies and calculate a wide range of ratios to see how the figures compare with what the textbooks and others in the industry produce prescribe. They occasionally also have meetings with finance directors and talk to experts in the industry. Hardly any have industrial or managerial experience. Thus their reports on companies and industry are useful fodder for journalists writing about company results, but only provide intermittent help in picking investments.

Annual general meeting

More than a century of legislation has piled on companies a mass of obligations to shareholders, many discharged at annual meetings. Yet private shareholders ignore or are ignorant of their rights and this widespread apathy permits management to drift into arrogance and incompetence.

A general meeting of shareholders must be held in each calendar year, with no more than 15 months between meetings. The board must there explain performance during the previous year and prospects for the current one, and shareholders must have the accounts and warning of the meeting 21 days in advance. Information available should include a register of directors' share dealings, and their service contracts.

Meetings provide a chance to question directors. But questions are rare, except from the occasional eccentric and obsessive, so curious events go unremarked. Chairmen can be brusque and unhelpful but shareholders seldom back people who do try to speak up for them, preferring to get quickly at the free drinks rather than investigate the conduct of business.

Shareholders can impose penalties at the meeting by their votes on the election and re-election of directors, appointment and pay of auditors, and the adoption of accounts. In practice, apathy by private investors and passivity by institutions means few rights are exercised.

Annual percentage rate

See True percentage rate of interest.

Annuity

Income receivable for a specified period or for life, secured by the payment of an initial sum. Rates depend on prevailing interest levels and the expected life-span of the recipient. Often the basis of a pension.

Anti-trust

It might be imagined that trust in the business world is in such short supply that everybody would encourage its growth. But in the United States restrictive practices such as monopolies or cartels used to be organized by a board of trustees with companies' shares being exchanged for the trust's certificates. The name has stuck, and with it the mistrust. The Sherman Anti-Trust Act of 1890, Clayton Act of 1914, Robinson Paxman Act of 1936, Milletydings Act 1937 and Celler Kefauver Act 1950 made life hard for big business.

Most notable have been the split into three of Du Pont at the beginning of the twentieth century, the breaking up of Standard Oil in 1911, and the fragmentation of AT&T's Bell telephone system. But the vague wording of the legislation has made enforcement problematic and open to protracted litigation.

Anton Piller order

An ingenious legal device which allows a plaintiff a surprise raid on the other side's premises to inspect or even remove documents and other evidence if they have convinced a court in secret hearing that the evidence might otherwise be destroyed. Often used in breach of copyright cases. Named after the German company first allowed it in a Court of Appeal decision: *Anton Piller v Manufacturing Processes Ltd* (1976) Ch 55.

APR

The Annual Percentage Rate of interest charged to consumers as defined by the Consumer Credit Act – see True rate of interest.

Arbitrage

Every shopper knows that prices are not the same even in adjacent shops. That applies to financial goods as well, though not for long.

Sharp businesspeople are quick to exploit discrepancies. If the dollar were cheaper in Zurich than London, it might be worth buying in Switzerland and selling swiftly in London before anyone notices. Similarly, if the price of a share varied between London and New York, one could trade between the two exchanges and make a quick killing.

It does not have to be international. If the cost of money from banks or from issuing Eurobonds is lower than the interest paid by local authorities or the money market, the shrewd financier will borrow from one and lend to the other. Taking such advantage of such differences is called arbitrage. Some large-scale US stock market operators call themselves arbitrageurs, but probably inaccurately.

'A' shares

See Non-voting shares.

Asset stripping

Making money is easier than making things, so when the share prices soar, take-over fever strikes. Acquisitions are often of sluggish companies and the new owner sells off its patents, successful offshoots, property and other assets to make a profit on the deal. That is classic asset stripping. Sometimes, some businesses are retained and, with new management, turned into profitable enterprises.

The activity provokes resentment, especially from employees, who may jib at being bought and sold, or put out of work. The advantage is that it keeps management alert to avoid the predator. The disadvantages are that managers avoid long-term investment, which may weaken the immediate position and so make them vulnerable; and such activity distracts from the production of wealth, relying on the shuffling of paper by sharp dealers.

Asset value

If a company goes under and its assets are sold for the benefit of creditors, the amount after paying holders of preference shares is called its net equity assets. That is what holders of ordinary shares would get. Complex accounting conventions mean the figure is hard to calculate, especially in valuing goodwill, stocks, and work in progress. In practice there is seldom anything left for equity holders after liquidation.

If net asset per share (surplus of assets over liabilities, divided by the number of shares on issue) is much higher than the share price, the company presents an open invitation to a bidder as the buyer would get assets on the cheap. Even if value is less than share price – as it should be to show that a company is worth more than the forced sale of its bits and pieces – the result depends on the assets being correctly valued.

There is also net current asset value, which indicates tightness of financial control. The figure is worked out by taking short-term assets (cash in bank, debtors, stocks, work in progress) and deducting current liabilities (creditors, overdraft, other short-term borrowings). The result should be negative, and the final debit should roughly equal one year's pre-tax profit. Anything much greater shows weak financial control so the company could be strapped for cash; much less and it is undergeared.

Association of Futures Brokers and Dealers

One of the original bodies under the Securities and Investments Board to supervise its part of the City. It merged to create the Securities and Futures Authority, which in turn was superseded by the Financial Services Authority.

At the money

A call option whose exercise price is about the same as the market price of the underlying security.

Auditor

Annual corporate accounts are produced by the company and attested by the directors, with auditors checking them for plausibility and adherence to rules set by legislation, the Stock

Exchange and the accountancy profession. So the auditor is just a watchdog, not a bloodhound in search of mischief and, apart from random samples, seldom goes back to verify the origin of figures or the business behind them. This causes much public anguish when companies go under, with arguments and litigation over how far the watchdog should sniff. It is a trade-off. The more auditors check the longer it takes and the more it costs. And some information has to be taken on trust unless they are to manage the company. Some auditors have also been gullible or disinclined to tangle with managers who in practice hire and pay them. In theory, auditors are appointed by shareholders, but they work with directors and even advise them to help prepare accounts. Accountants have enforced ever greater disclosure; consequently, annual accounts are stuffed with so much complex data that only specialists can elicit the facts from them.

Authorized share capital

The amount of shares (of all classes) that a company is allowed to issue is specified in the memorandum of association, and it takes a shareholder meeting to change the figure. Not all of it has to be issued.

Automated teller machines

In the US bank clerks and cashiers are called tellers, so the cash dispenser becomes an automatic teller machine. The full phrase is used mainly in the US, but ATM is a common contraction for the equipment elsewhere as well. Originally the label distinguished it from cash dispensers, which did nothing else, but as the equipment became more sophisticated the distinction became meaningless.

Average

Contrary to instinctive suspicions, statisticians, politicians, civil servants and journalists are not always intentionally misleading in the way they use figures, but one does need to know just what they mean. Averages are a good example.

In statistics there are three measures for getting the central figure in a series: mean, mode and median. The one called average in most normal speech is the arithmetic mean – ie adding up all the items (say wages) and dividing the total by the number of items (number of wage earners).

This often reveals little and can sometimes mislead – eg a few employees might be getting such astronomical pay as to overwhelm the substantial number at the bottom of the scale. That could produce the old paradox/joke that most people are getting less than average pay.

The median might be a better guide because that is the figure at which half the items are on either side. Mode is the most commonly occurring figure in a series.

For some statistics with a bell-shaped distribution (frequency on the vertical axis and size of items on horizontal) the three types of average are close together. But when distribution is skewed more information is necessary.

Averaging

If the price of a share falls below the price paid for it, an investor can buy more and so reduce the average cost per share. This is called pound cost averaging. It can be dangerous if merely reducing average cost since every purchase should really be a rational decision in its own right.

Avoidance

In normal usage avoidance and evasion mean much the same, but the tax authorities have traditionally defined avoidance to mean legal non-payment of tax through making the most of provisions and loopholes in the legislation to claim every allowance and relief available.

As Lord President Clyde said in 1929:

> No man in this country is under the smallest obligation, moral or other, so to arrange his legal relations to his business or to his property as to enable the Inland Revenue to put the largest possible shovel into his stores. The Inland Revenue is not slow, and quite rightly, to take every advantage which is open to it under the taxing statutes for the purpose of depleting the taxpayer's pocket. And the taxpayer is, in like manner, entitled to be astute to prevent, so far as he honestly can, the depletion of his means by the Revenue.

In the United States, Judge Learned Hand agreed:

> Over and over again courts have said that there is nothing sinister in so arranging one's affairs to keep taxes as low as possible. Everybody does so, rich or poor, and all do right for nobody owes any public duty to pay more than the law demands; taxes are enforced exactions, not voluntary contributions. To demand more in the name of morals is mere cant.

Criminal non-payment of what the law demands is called evasion by the Inland Revenue.

Avoidance

Backwardation

Financial terms with several different meanings make life very difficult for the non-expert.

The most common meaning of backwardation was traditionally the payment by the seller of shares to a buyer who permits late delivery. It is quoted as so much per share, say 2p, and compensates the purchaser for foregoing their rights to delivery of the shares on the date that rules say he should have them.

It is most common as a form of bear equivalent of contango (qv). In other words, a speculator has decided the price of a share is about to fall. They sell shares they do not own (in the hope of picking them up more cheaply before the need for delivery) and make a profit on the difference. If things do not work out quite right but the investor decides the timing was only slightly out, they can ask for the deal to be carried forward. For that they pay a price: backwardation.

A more common current usage in the stock market describes what happens in fast-moving markets when the market-makers move their prices rapidly. Occasionally, one market-maker's bid price (at which they buy shares) is higher than another's offer price (at which they sell), which is the wrong way around and permits sharp operators a quick deal between them and at a small profit. It is usually rectified pretty smartly. The word is also sometimes used to describe a higher spot price for a commodity than a forward price.

Balance of payments

A popular, crude and not always reliable indicator of a nation's success or economic health. It is the comparatively small difference between the very large sums of imports and exports and includes flows of cash which can overwhelm the sums and make the final figure all but meaningless. For instance, if UK interest rates are high, cash from overseas inflates the positive side. The aim may have been to improve trade figures, support the currency or contain money supply, but the effect is to raise the cost of borrowing for domestic industrialists, and it eventually produces outflows of interest. Capital inflow is also inflated by corporate overseas borrowing. The balance of trade omits capital flows but it is useful to separate invisible exports, especially for Britain, which has seldom seen a positive balance on visible trade in the past 100 years. Invisibles such as shipping, insurance, banking, patents, royalties, tourism, air transport and dividends from overseas investment have helped offset the visible deficit.

Obviously, not every country can run a surplus – one person's debt is another's credit – and, for instance, the outflow of US dollars fuelled much of world trade growth after World War II. But if a country ran persistently large and growing deficits, other countries would be subsidizing its economy, which makes them disgruntled and they might start worrying about its stability. The currency then falls, making imports dearer and exports cheaper, which should automatically correct the problem.

Balance sheet

Annual reports of companies contain a profit and loss account and a balance sheet. The former describes how it traded through the year, the latter tots up its financial position on the last day of its year. It may not be a representative day, figures may have been manipulated for apparent health or tax, and by the time shareholders get it the sums are old. Being a record of the past, the figures are at best an uncertain guide to the future.

They show assets and liabilities and the table is called a balance sheet because they are defined to be equal. Assets will include items like factory, machinery etc, which are integral part of the company. Sometimes there is an item called good-will, which is odd (especially if being depreciated), but proba-bly is the relic of buying a company for more than its asset value, and the extra had somehow to be accounted for. Current assets include cash and near-cash like bank balance, money owed by customers, stocks, work in progress and the like. Liabilities include the share capital (although in practice this is hardly ever repaid), other capital issues like debenture and loan stocks, overdrafts, money owed to creditors and so on. Surplus of current assets over current liabilities is the company's work-ing capital.

Baltic Exchange

One of the many City institutions which grew out of a 17th-cen-tury coffee house – from two, to be exact. One was the Virginia and Maryland Coffee House, which from 1744 was known as the Virginia and Baltick because captains trading to the American colonies and the Baltic seaboard used to meet there to arrange business.

The other was the Jerusalem Coffee House, which by 1891 had evolved in the London Shipping Exchange. In 1903 the two moved into a joint building as the Baltic Mercantile and Shipping Exchange. That begins to show its function – the Baltic was retained from nostalgia.

As the name implies it has two functions. The mercantile part deals in commodities – mainly grain, oilseeds and soya bean – and is a sort of retail end of the Corn Exchange (the large-scale dealing centre for cereals, founded in 1749) and has developed a sophisticated futures (qv) market.

The shipping part is the largest market in the world for deal-ing in cargo space and vessel chartering, in particular tramp ship cargoes. There is also a big market in second-hand ships. A rising portion is in air cargo and plane chartering but much of that is done over the telephone or telex rather than on the floor of the Baltic Exchange.

Big growth markets in shipping have been containers, and bulk carriers and tankers which are signed on long charter even before being built. That means another part of the business bypasses the exchange.

Bank

Only institutions vetted and approved by the Financial Services Authority are allowed to call themselves banks.

Bank for International Settlements

Originally set up to administer debt repayments among European countries in the 1920s, the bank has more recently been organizing international discussions on finance separated from politics. The talking shop for European central bankers meets once a month at Basel. It still also does a little Eurodollar business to implement the members' collective decision.

Bank of England

The UK's central bank, first set up by royal charter from William and Mary in 1694. Its nickname, The Old Lady of Threadneedle Street, came from a 1797 Gillray cartoon.

The Bank was privately owned until the 1946 nationalization. It represents the City to government and it is government in the City. Although it had legal powers over financial institutions, especially banks, most of its supervision was behind the scenes ('the governor's eyebrows'). For instance, during the sorting out of the Blue Arrow scandal in 1989, the Bank suggested quietly that some of the National Westminster Bank people were not acceptable and all resigned – one against whom an official report found no evidence was nevertheless barred from City jobs. This part of its supervision was, however, taken over by the Financial Services Authority.

It is also responsible for issuing currency, it issues gilts for government, stabilizes exchange rates by intervention in the markets, and sets interest rates.

Being an independent voice on the economy of the country, there is often friction between the Bank and the Treasury. That was removed from open conflict when the government in 1997 gave the bank the right to set interest rates, for which the Monetary Policy Committee (qv) was set up to meet once a month.

Bankruptcy

Individuals totally incapable of paying their debts are bankrupt (companies go into receivership or liquidation (qv)).

Legally it happens when the creditors run out of patience and insist on their cash. Sometimes people use bankruptcy as a devious way of evading creditors while keeping their belongings. But that is getting harder.

Barter

Exchanging goods and services rather than using money. It works quite well in primitive societies, but every attempt to revive it in modern times has failed because a relative value still has to be set on what is being traded. In modern times its most frequent use is by poor countries short of the hard currencies needed to buy advanced industrial goods. So, for example, airliners are paid for in jam, cloth or raw materials, and steel plants may be paid for in the steel they produce. Also called switch deals.

Base rate

Heavily overdrawn customers paying through the nose will think the base rate well named. It is in fact the rate of interest set by the banks on which they base the rates for loans and deposits. The level is set at what the banks think they can get away with, so it is related to money markets, which in turn are influenced by minimum lending rate (qv). There is no collusion but none of the big four clearers – Barclays, National Westminster, Lloyds and Midland – gets out of line for more than a day or two.

Local authorities and state organizations might get away with paying 0.5 per cent over base for overdrafts, blue chip companies might have to go to 1 per cent, and so on. Impoverished private customers and small business can expect to be charged anything from 3 to 5 per cent over, depending on luck and bargaining ability. If one puts cash into the bank as seven-day money one would generally get 1.5 per cent under base rate. Money on three-month call is nearer the prevailing money market rates.

Basis point

When massive amounts of money are at stake even tiny differences in interest or currency conversion rate can make huge differences. That is why in the big-finance businesses they measure the changes in basis points, which are hundredth of a per cent. So the difference between a bond yielding 7.83 per cent and another yielding 8.26 per cent is 53 basis points.

Bear

See Bulls and bears.

Bear raid

A sudden unprovoked attack on a share by speculators. They indulge in selling large blocks of visible shares, which depresses the share price and this is a bear raid. If it is not provoked by a sudden panic about the company's prospects but a devious ploy to acquire shares more cheaply, these speculators will wait until the price has spiralled down and then buy steadily and stealthily before the market notices that the buyers have returned.

Bear squeeze

If somebody is a bear – ie thinks the market or a specific share is going to fall – one tactic is to 'go short', ie to sell more shares than one has. Then, as the shares fall during the fortnightly account, one can buy them back at a lower price before the need for delivery, and so make a nice profit.

Unfortunately, it is not always so neat. If the price starts rising during this speculative period the bear can deliver only by balancing their position at the higher price. Then they will be badly squeezed because the price is already rising against them but through their own buying the price is likely to rise even further. Closing such bear positions can have a marked effect on prices of some shares.

Sometimes, market-makers suspect that bears are at work, artificially depressing a price, and will then squeeze them by lifting prices at the right psychological moment.

Bearer bond

Most shares are registered with the issuing company, which means that the company therefore knows who owns the business. Even if investors try to hide behind nominee holdings (qv) the company has the right to ask for the beneficial owner. But bearer bonds change hands without registration and dividends are paid to whoever claims them. Such bonds are rare.

Bed and breakfast

This is a Stock Exchange term but it does not mean they have finally found a use for the abandoned trading floor and started taking in lodgers. It is a brief transit through the market, but only financially.

Capital gains tax is levied on the amount a share has appreciated between buying and selling, above a minimum threshold. To get the maximum benefit of the annual threshold exemption, a shrewd investor sells soaring shares held and buys them back at the same price. Then next year's tax calculation will be started again at the higher price. The market people take just a notional fee.

In theory the shares are sold one evening after hours and bought back at the start of business next morning, bedding in the exchange overnight. For companies longer term stays of a month have to be arranged.

The 1998 Budget cancelled that dodge, so the alternative of 'bed and partner' was invented, allowing, say, the husband to sell his shares one night and his wife to buy them back the following day.

Beta coefficient

A measure of a share's volatility – how much more or less its price moves compared with the market as a whole. The bigger the beta, the greater is sensitivity to movements generally. For instance, a beta of 1.4 means the share has moved 40 per cent more than the index over the past five years.

Bid/offer spread

See Spread.

Big Bang

In October 1986 the Stock Exchange abandoned the traditional working methods it had fought for decades to preserve. Three main changes arrived: outside ownership of brokers and jobbers (renamed market-makers); broking and market-making within the same firm (the exchange had long said that could damage investor protection); and negotiated commissions.

Centuries of tradition and established working practices were swept away to appease quangos, which scrutinize restrictive practices, and in an attempt to make London a world centre for trading and money making.

Three of the most immediate results were the purchase of most large stockbrokers and jobbers by financial conglomerates (many of them foreign), the disappearance of the stock market floor as trading went electronic, and a sharp rise in costs for small investors.

Bill broker

In theory, this is someone who trades in bills of exchange (qv), who could be acting on their own account or as an intermediary. In practice, the terms tends to be synonymous with discount houses (qv) who act on their behalf.

Bill of exchange

A written undertaking to pay a specified sum of money – like a cheque – usually post-dated. The recipient can endorse the paper and pass it on for their own payments so long as the original signer (called an acceptor because they accept liability) is reckoned to be financially sound. It is also possible to exchange them for cash, but as they are not exchangeable for money until the set date, discount houses (qv) which specialize in buying bills charge for such early payments from their own resources. Banks also sometimes discount bills.

Billions

There was a time when we talked with awe of thousands of dollars, much less pounds, and a millionaire was rich and rare. A sign of the times is the increasing frequency of billions. Unhappily, there is no standard billion. Americans, who already have a smaller gallon (we have the imperial measure, which even sounds bigger) and weaker proof spirit, have smaller billions as well. Theirs is a thousand million, while a British billion is a million million. To confuse matters further, there has been a fashion in recent years for using US billions – even the Treasury and several heavy newspapers have succumbed – which is confusing.

It is a mistake, because inflation will call on steadily larger numbers. Americans have already moved on to trillions (an English billion), while an English trillion, however, is a million English billions. As if that were not confusing enough, Americans also have zillions, the Continentals have milliards (US billions), and in India there is the lakh (100 000) and crore (ten millions). Perhaps it would best to go for the undisputed scientific notation of 10 raised to the requisite power. So a million is 10^6 and a British billion would be 10^{12}, and everybody would know the number of noughts involved.

Black days

Several of the days have acquired notoriety for market plunges in a long history of market disasters. For instance, Black Monday was 19 October 1987 when most of the world's major stock exchanges plunged by record amounts. Black Tuesday was 29 October 1929, the worst day of the world economic collapse which came to be called the Great Crash. Black Wednesday was 9 September 1992 when Sterling could no longer withstand the general incredulity at its conversion rate to other European currencies, despite pouring most of the country's reserves into a Canute-like attempt to convince them, and the UK was forced to abandon the European Exchange Rate Mechanism.

Black economy

The shady end of entrepreneurial enterprise: the traders and craftsmen who work for cash and do not declare the amount for income tax, corporation tax, or VAT. By definition, it is hard to measure but it has been estimated at over £20 000 million a year.

Billions

Blue button

When the Stock Exchange had a trading floor, clerks working for stockbrokers needed identification to gain admission and a distinctive blue badge to show they were not authorized to trade. Hence their nickname.

Blue chips

A US expression originally derived (appropriately enough) from gambling where the highest value chips were coloured blue. Now it denotes the best and safest form of equity, usually in large companies. The 100 companies in the FT-SE 100 Index are reckoned to be blue chips. But that too is a warning: British Leyland, Polly Peck and Rolls-Royce were Index stocks until they went bust.

Bond

One of those modish words which become popular and are then applied to almost anything, which is why most traditional dictionaries are misleading about this. The word conjures up safety ('My word is my ...'), Agent 007, or sado-masochism depending on one's tastes, but in finance it is generally used to give a feeling of security to a variety of investments in the way the word 'gold' is often brought in to suggest opulence. Local authority bonds are fixed-interest securities redeemed within one to five years, and are similar to gilt-edged securities (qv) issued by central government, except for the absence of a secondary market. Yearling bonds, however, are issued by a couple of hundred local authorities to last one year (and are replaced with a new issue on maturity) also on a fixed-interest basis, but are traded on the Stock Exchange.

National Savings, on the other hand, issues variable interest bonds: capital which rolls up interest, and income, which operate in practice in a way similar to bank accounts as investors can get their money out at any time. Then there are Premium Bonds, which merely give monthly prizes like a lottery. Guaranteed income bonds from life assurance companies are a tax-efficient fixed-interest investment on a one- to five-year basis. Property and commodity bonds are, in effect, single premium insurance contracts (the latter offshore). Finally, there are bonds issued by overseas governments, which are also fixed-interest redeemable securities analogous to gilts. US ones are usually redeemed after ten years.

Some of the ancient versions from overthrown governments such as czarist Russia or imperial China now have purely decorative value, being issues that have splendid engraving and pretty colours but are unlikely to be redeemed or receive interest.

Bonus issues

A parcel of free shares, dropped into the surprised investor's lap by a company in which they own shares, is called a bonus or capitalization issue (see Scrip). For tax the bonus issue shares are taken to have been acquired at the same as the original holding.

Boom

Rapid economic expansion, increasing production, rising living standards, growing investment, and falling employment represent economic boom. In Britain it has more often produced a burst of ill-balanced growth trailing trade deficits, inflation, higher interest rates and devalued currency. It may be fear of all that which makes Chancellors of the Exchequer start damping things down before they roar away, but in any case ecologists would probably point out the accelerating depletion of the earth's resources and greed in a world full of hunger. Nothing is free of guilt any more.

Bourse

French for Stock Exchange and sometimes used as a label for other stock markets.

Bretton Woods

In July 1944 the then 44 members of the United Nations gathered in the small New Hampshire town of Bretton Woods to build a better post-war financial world, not reliant on gold and free from the shocks of large currency movements.

Currencies were fixed or allowed 'managed flexibility' to prevent competitive devaluations or destabilization by speculators. That would give businesspeople assurance about the value of future foreign exchange earnings.

Two institutions would oversee the new order: the World Bank (qv), which is a fund, and the International Monetary Fund (qv), which is a bank.

To some extent, and for a time, it worked as international trade did flourish and currencies did become convertible. But its rigidities caused its downfall. The careful process of setting exchange rates was submerged in floated currencies. In addition, the outflow of US dollars helped lubricate world trade but eventually started worrying financiers and faith in the dollar was undermined. As the dollar was keystone to the graceful Bretton Woods arch, its removal caused the collapse of the agreement. The two institutions spawned by the conference still live and do their part to iron out world financial problems.

Bridging loan

Borrowing that spans a short period between immediate need and the time when a proper long-term facility can be arranged.

Broker

The stock market does not want any stray investor poking into its computers so the punter must pass instructions to a stockbroker, who will then key the requisite instructions into the electronics. It comforts the authorities that they can supervise a small number of brokers.

Building societies

Originally formed to build homes for members, these became savings clubs providing loans to enable non-members as well to buy their homes. A simple system pays interest on deposits and charges for the safest of long-term loans.

Mergers have gradually reduced the number of societies from 2 286 in 1900 to about 70 now, though the number of members is still as high as 16 million, with assets growing from £60 million to nearly £140 billion.

From the late 1970s the banks realized what opportunities they had been missing and entered the mortgage market, to be joined later by other financial institutions. This came just at the time when the market began to approach saturation – when over two-thirds of homes were owner occupied the market looked ready to contract, so building societies wanted to move into the areas from which their competitors started.

Societies are supervised by a Building Societies Commission and a statutory ombudsman service to hear complaints. A protection scheme guarantees that at least 90 per cent of deposits up to £10 000 are repaid if a society fails.

The 1986 Building Societies Act permitted societies to widen activities into giving overdrafts and chequebooks, as well as selling insurance, Personal Equity Plans, pension policies and unit trusts shares, and owning estate agencies. They can also turn into limited liability companies and many took the logical step of converting into banks, persuading their owners to permit the move by bribing them with large offers of money and shares.

Bulldog bonds

Nobody seems very sure why a bond issued in London by an overseas government agency should be called a bulldog, since the only British thing about them is the sterling denomination. But then similar bonds denominated in dollars and issued in New York are called Yankees, and the Tokyo issues are called Samurais.

The Stock Exchange prefers to restrict the term to paper guaranteed by an overseas government, or international body in which Britain has an interest. The rest of the City uses the term for any debenture-like issue even if coming from a commercial organization. Convertibles, however, are excluded. Bulldogs returned to fashion after the 1979 abolition of exchange control. To prevent a flood of safe bonds upsetting the British government's manipulation of the gilts market, the Bank of England regulates the volume of issues. But the bureaucracy soon made them unpopular because the relatively cheap and unregulated Eurobond market was preferable.

Bulls and bears

The bulls and bears of the stock market's curious bestiary seem to have originated in the 18th century. There are also stags (qv), lame ducks (qv), and of course there is no shortage of sharks. Many reasons have been suggested for the origins of the terms. One theory suggests comparisons with the huntsman who sold the skin before the bear was even killed (nowadays this is called 'going short'); another says it is just a corruption of bare, in the sense of being devoid of stock; some say it comes from the fact that bears knock people down while bulls toss them in the air; and John Bull was a portly optimist. Whatever the derivation, around the world a bull is an optimist and bull markets rise, while bears are gloomy and bear markets fall. So when market-makers are bullish about a company they 'go long' (take some shares onto their own books), but if they are bearish they 'go short' (sell shares they do not own on the assumption they will have picked them up cheaper before the time comes for delivery).

Business cycle

See Cycle.

Call

Another of those portmanteau financial words which is dangerously flexible with several unrelated meanings.

Sometimes shares are issued on a stock market version of the never-never, though the City calls it nil-paid or partly-paid basis. It means one has put up nothing, or only part of the money, at the start of the issue, but at a specified date the rest becomes payable when the amount is at call. In a different sense of the word, money at call is cash loaned with the facility for immediate withdrawal.

A call option is the right to acquire shares (to call the equity) at a price agreed now though the transaction will be at some specified date in the future (see Options).

Cancellation period

See Cooling off.

Capital/current account

The balance of payments (qv) is simply the difference between what cash comes flowing into the country, and what flows out. To paraphrase Mr Micawber: exports £1 000 million, imports £1 005 million – result: misery. That is the current account. It includes visible trade (imports and exports of goods) and invisibles (income and payment for services, plus dividends).

On top of that comes the cash deposited across boundaries, and investment flows. That is the capital account. The part on short-term loan and which can be recalled quickly is the 'hot money', which pursues interest rates and currency benefits around the globe. More tepid are shares and property invest-ments, and fairly cold is the industrial investment in factories and equipment. The net figure depends on the relative attraction of Britain as an investment haven.

Capitalization

The total value of a company on the stock market's assessment: the total market value of its shares. It is therefore easily calculated by multiplying the current share price by the number of shares on issue.

Capitalization issue

Formal description of bonus or scrip issue (qv).

Carat

The locust tree or carob has seeds which are remarkably consistent in weight and were therefore used by Indian Ocean pearl fishers as weights for selling their finds. The carob (called kirat by the Arabs) unit was later applied to gems and the word was gradually corrupted to carat. Originally it was $\frac{1}{144}$ of an ounce or $3\frac{1}{3}$ grains, but it varied depending on time and place. In 1932 the metric carat was standardized at 200mg (3.086 grain).

For more obscure (perhaps related) reasons, the fineness of gold is also called carat and related to the Roman siliqua, which was a twenty-fourth of Constantine's solidus coin. Hence, it still means the part in 24 that is gold – eg 24 carat is pure gold, and 18 carat is $\frac{18}{24}$ or 75 per cent gold.

Cards

Charge cards, such as American Express, not only charge for holding the plastic but also demand full repayment immediately, and get shirty if the money is not rapidly paid. Credit cards, such as MasterCard and Visa, provide credit at a price, and sometimes provide the card free.

Cartel

When a small group of companies dominates a market (see Oligopoly), there is a temptation to avoid unprofitable competition by rigging the trade. Strictly, a cartel should entail pooling some resources, such as setting up a central selling organization, but it usually just involves agreements to control output, regulate prices, or divide home or export markets.

This can be within a country (eg the German steel cartel of the 1930s headed by Krupp, or the British cement market after the war), organized internationally by multinational corporations, or even recognized by governments (Organization of Petroleum Exporting Countries (OPEC), International Air Transport Association).

When the cartel's sole aim is to keep up prices, it arouses antagonism and rapidly becomes unstable as members think they can benefit from breaking ranks (more efficient ones cut prices to get more of the market). In other words, the members find it more profitable to cheat their partners than their customers. OPEC is a good example, as are some of the commodity agreements.

Countries control cartels as other monopolies and restrictive practices – for complicated historical reasons, Americans call cartels 'trusts', so their controls are called anti-trust laws (qv).

Cash and new

Some stock market transactions are arranged with the explicit intention for the shares to be delivered late. That means, in effect, the seller gets credit for those days. If at the agreed time of delivery the seller is still not ready to hand over the shares (because, for instance, the price has not dropped enough for them to pick them up cheaper), for a fee the broker organizes another contract for later delivery. That is usually done by closing the contract and opening another at a slightly different price.

Cash flow

In companies it is as important to know how cash is flowing through the enterprise as it is to check the profit: sales may be booming and cash flow apparently healthy, but in reality the company is making disastrous losses; conversely, profits may look fine but people are so slow paying that the company founders because it cannot pay debts or even wages. As so often in finance, the expression has several uses. Financial journalists mean profit plus depreciation, though at best this gives only a rough idea of cash resources. Another definition is the difference between cash in and cash out through a period, and this is what accountants mean when appraising prospects. Growing businesses pay out more than they get in because they buy stock, have work in progress and fixed assets, and the negative cash flow produces an overdraft. A company slowing down can have an embarrassingly high liquidity as the cash floods in with no profitable investment.

Businesses evaluate investment through cash flow, usually discounting future receipts (because it is worth less than cash in hand which can be invested). This produces the net present value of a sum to be received in the future. Finding the correct discounting factor (based on inflation and interest rates over the period) is tricky and the cash flows are only estimates, but it is still better than a blind guess.

Caveat emptor

This is an ancient maxim of English law which supposed that purchasers are not complete idiots, but if they do nevertheless buy foolishly they should be prepared to accept the consequences of their incompetence. Hence the Latin tag – meaning let the buyer beware – which implied that the seller was not obliged to point out the defects in their goods.

The rule is now defunct because governments feel we need constant protection from ourselves, not being clever enough to withstand sharp salesmen. The buyer is now pretty safe but the seller had better be careful.

Any seller is now in constant danger of transgressing legislation such as the Sale of Goods Act, Consumer Protection Act, two Hire Purchase Acts, Trades Description Act, Defective Premises Act, Supply of Goods (Implied Terms) Act, Unfair Contract Terms Act, Weights and Measures Act, Food and Drugs Act, Consumer Credit Act, Supply of Goods and Services Act, Prevention of Fraud (Investments) Act, Financial Services Act, and so on. Plus, of course, a weight of subsequent case law.

Additionally, responsibility is to be placed on the manufacturer by strict liability, which makes it responsible for damages caused by its goods even if it was not negligent and was as careful as it was reasonable for it to be. The cost of all this is, of course, borne by consumers in higher costs, as closing each tiny loophole adds to the cost of production and the bureaucracy piles up the cost of administration.

Central bank

The institution at the centre of a country's monetary and financial system. In England it is the Bank of England (qv), in the United States it is the Federal Reserve, in Germany the Bundesbank, and so on. Among their jobs are acting as banker to the government, arranging for the issuing of government stock such as gilts, and acting as banker to the commercial banking system in the country. In some countries they also supervise the banking system, print and issue the currency. In Europe the work of the national institutions will be largely taken over by a central organization as part of the monetary union.

Certificates of deposit (CD)

Banknotes were born when renaissance jewellers/ bankers issued certificates that the bearer had deposited gold in the vaults. The idea seems to have caught on, yet it took until 1966 for the money market to produce the corporate version – the certificate of deposit. That was the London dollar CD, and two years later sterling was added. Companies with, say, £500 000 temporarily lying idle put it on deposit. The longer it is agreed to be left the higher the interest, so the company may undertake to leave it a year. In return it gets a receipt – a certificate of deposit – stating the amount, the interest and the length of time on deposit. Cash needed earlier than expected may not be withdrawn, but the CD can be sold to a discount house (qv). Some deals are also done through stockbrokers, money brokers and banks. The price depends on the interest related to the prevailing market rate. Confusingly, the discount house gets the money from the banks to buy the CD. But this is just another example of cash swishing round fast enough to ensure that none of it ever lies idle for a second.

Everybody is happy: the company gets the cash it needs, the bank has dependable long-term money, and the discount house makes a small profit every time the money passes through its hands.

Some £5 000 million of sterling CDs are outstanding.

Chapter 11

A portion of the US legislation Bankruptcy Reform Act 1978 that enables a company to be protected from irate unpaid creditors while the managers reorganize in the hope of becoming a viable business. The British have tried to emulate the procedure with administration orders (qv).

Charts

City chartists have little in common with Cobden and Bright of the 19th-century franchise movement. That was a campaign for human dignity, the current charts serve the more mundane purpose of making money.

The theory behind financial charts was evolved by Charles H Dow (who helped found Dow Jones and the *Wall Street Journal*), at the end of the 19th century. He noticed that graphs of share price movements followed patterns that were regular enough to allow predictions of how the pattern would continue, and hence what the price of a share would be. There are primary trends – general bull or bear markets – which can last several years. Important rallies or declines interrupting the smooth primary lines are called secondary reactions and can last for up to three months. Tertiary movements are daily fluctuations.

To forecast, the pattern must be identified, and these have graphic descriptive names. 'Head and shoulders' is a peak flanked either side by smaller peaks, and presages a fall; conversely, a 'reversed head and shoulders' heralds a rise. There are also 'support areas' and 'resistance areas' (levels from which price tends to rebounce), plus 'triangles', 'trend lines', 'channels', 'double tops' and so on.

Sceptics produce mathematical models which suggest that share price movements are random in the way tossing a coin has a random outcome – in fact charting heads and tails produced very similar lines. But that ignores the vital time element.

Charts do conform to psychological observations of behaviour patterns but still require subjective interpretation, which makes them less scientific and more subject to skill. For people contemplating investment, they do at least add an extra dimension to share analysis.

Extrapolation

Chinese walls

Since stockbrokers, fund managers, financial advisers and mar-ket-makers can exist within the same firm, the potential for conflicts of interest is obvious. Separate parts of the organiza-tion are supposed to ignore the financial welfare of the group and act only within their own fields of interest.

Keeping apart these complementary functions to ensure the customer is not cheated, is a system of 'Chinese walls', presumably on the theory that a 1400 mile wall which kept out the Mongols must be good. We should have known better: the original was expensive and conspicuous but ineffective.

The City walls are patrolled by compliance officers, but detected cases of insider trading in recent years shows the walls to be permeable and in need of repointing. Even then, few people are confident that they can ever be effective.

Churning

Stockbrokers earn their money from commission on trading. They care little whether clients are buying or selling but they certainly make no profit on clients keeping their money in a selected investment, no matter how sound. During hard times therefore they may be tempted to goad clients into trading whether that improves the portfolio or not. This is called churning.

City code

See Take-Over Panel.

City Panel on Take-Overs and Mergers

See Take-Over Panel.

Clawback

One meaning is for the loss of tax reliefs when later events cancel the eligibility of transactions and the Inland Revenue asks for the cash. Another is the right of existing shareholders in a company to have access to newly issued shares even after they have been taken up by financial institutions – an underwriter may therefore agree to return any shares subscribed for by existing holders.

Close company

Legal definition of a company controlled by (ie they hold more than half the shares) no more than five people or one which is controlled by directors (even if there are more than five of them). The concept was devised to stop a small band of owners rolling up dividends in the company to provide a lower-tax capital gain. So if a close company does not distribute a minimum percentage of profits as dividend, it will be assessed at tax rates as if it had done so. In the United States it is called a closed company.

Closed end fund

The end that is closed is the one that issues shares. So, with a fixed number of shares, investors wanting to get shares have to buy in the secondary market, for instance the stock exchange. This is an investment trust. A unit trust on the other hand continues to issue units to any new investor wanting to take part.

Codicil

A legally-binding postscript to a will. As with the will itself, the signature to it must be properly witnessed.

Coincident indicators

There are series of financial statistics which provide an indication of where a country's economy is or where it is going. The coincident indicators like industrial production or unemployment show what the current position is – or as nearly up to date as the publication of the figures. The ones which purport to predict are called leading indicators, and the ones which confirm the past are called lagging indicators.

Cold call

Uninvited offers of investments are illegal. Investors have to warm the relationship first by asking the seller for information or advice, or by offering to put in money. The Securities and Investments Board (qv) and its brood of self-regulatory organizations control such activities and licence financial intermediaries. If any break the rules by cold calling, the SIB should be informed.

Comecon

The Soviet equivalent of the Common Market was the Council for Mutual Economic Assistance, called Comecon for short. Members were Bulgaria, Czechoslovakia, East Germany, Hungary, Mongolia, Poland, Rumania and the Soviet Union. Since its dissolution, several of the members are trying to join the European Union instead.

Commercial paper

Part of the trend toward securitisation (qv), which allows companies to issue paper which is not quite shares but which is negotiable since it can be readily bought and sold. It counts as debt and may be issued by listed companies with net assets of over £50 million for maturity between 7 and 364 days in chunks of at least £500 000 through banks which charge a commission for the service. While the security is on issue, the company must make monthly returns to the Bank of England, which also details how much is currently on issue.

Commodities

Economics has several definitions of this word but in the context of the City it describes raw materials used by industry and traded on specialist markets. There are two types: 'soft', such as cocoa, coffee, tea, shellac, sisal, jute, sugar, soya, wool, corn (and, in Chicago, a range of other things like orange juice and pork bellies); and 'hard', which are metals like copper, tin, zinc, lead, aluminium, and silver.

They are dealt in as 'spot' for immediate delivery, and 'futures' (qv) for later delivery.

Common agricultural policy (CAP)

Apparently a misnomer, only the middle word being appropriate. The CAP is the European Union's co-ordination of farming production in a way calculated to produce butter, beef and egg mountains, to set beside the wine and milk lakes. The CAP then aggravates its mistake (and taxpayers) by selling off the surplus cheaply to places like Russia thus subsidizing foreign consumers rather than its own.

Such actions have negated in the public eye any good the rest of the EU may do, and have led to a series of vicious internal arguments.

Member states of the EU agree on prices of agricultural products, which are maintained by varying import levies so that food from outside the EU is never below threshold price. (Note the similarity to the British Corn Laws, which produced such violent controversy during the first half of the 19th century and were finally repealed to enable the poor to eat.) The European Commission keeps up domestic prices by buying produce when prices are below the threshold; which is how the mountains and lakes are produced. It also subsidizes exports when world prices and intervention prices are out of kilter. The CAP also involves the use of EU funds to modernize farms.

Common stock

US for ordinary shares.

Commutation

In financial circles the usual meaning is the specific swapping of entitlement to regular future pension payments in return for an immediate lump sum.

Company doctor

Ailing companies usually go through a traumatic period when creditors and shareholders desperately try to haul them back from the edge of death. One ploy is to pep up management by appointing an expert to bring new drive and ability to the board. This outsider, a person of proven management ability who has turned other companies round who is brought in to perform extensive surgery, is called a company doctor.

Comparative advantage

The principle laid down by David Ricardo at the beginning of the 19th century that every country has something it can produce cheapest. This had interesting consequences as he developed the notion – for example, one should concentrate on what one can do best even if there are things which one can do slightly better than others. Ricardo used the example of Portugal, which should export wine to buy cloth from Britain, even though the Portuguese can make cloth with slightly fewer hours of labour, because the extra effort put into wine more than offset the loss on cloth.

If making a unit of wine takes 80 hours of labour in Portugal and 120 hours in England, while a unit of cloth takes 90 hours of labour in Portugal and 100 in Britain, it looks as if Portugal has an absolute advantage in making the two (170 against 220). But a unit of Portuguese wine buys $\frac{8}{9}$ of Portuguese cloth (80:90 hours), and $1\frac{1}{5}$ British cloth (80:100), so it makes sense for Portugal to specialize in making wine and trading it for British textiles.

Composite interest rate

The Treasury sets a tax rate for banks and building societies to pay on interest-bearing accounts before crediting the customer and this is called the composite rate. It moves in line with income tax but remains slightly below the standard rate. As a result payers of standard rate gain a bit, but people who are not liable to tax lose because they cannot reclaim the interest deducted. For them, National Savings Bank is preferable because it pays dividends gross. Payers of higher rate tax are still liable for extra tax on the interest received.

Concert party

Forget pierrots on the pier, this is serious if devious City business. Usually at the time of a take-over it refers to a group of people or companies acting together. As a result, the City Code applying to individuals covers the whole group acting in concert, and dictates what they can do or say, how much of the company they may hold in what circumstances, and when specific actions become mandatory or forbidden.

Not to be confused with a fan club (qv), though to an outsider they do seem very similar.

Confederation of British Industry (CBI)

Formed in 1965 at government instigation by the merger of four management organizations. Membership covers some 250 000 of Britain's millions of companies, and about 220 employers or trade associations.

Conglomerate

A company which does not confine its activities to one type of business. A company which mines ore, smelts it, makes steel, produces screws and sells them through a chain of its retailers is vertically integrated. One that bakes cakes, makes jam, blends tea, produces stock cubes, and imports coffee is horizontally integrated in the food business. But a company that owns tankers, runs teashops, manufactures flagpoles, builds bungalows and makes digital hygrometers is a conglomerate.

Fashion swings ensure that conglomeration is sometimes considered sensible diversification, or spread of sound management, and sometimes aggressive take-overs creating large businesses for megalomania and greed.

Consols

Abbreviation for government consolidated stock – a gilt-edged security without a redemption date.

Constant prices

Would that they were. Expressing government statistics in 'constant prices' does not mean Whitehall thinks inflation does not exist or pretends it has been cured. On the contrary, it is a way of getting at real volume changes in consumer spending, production etc, by removing the inflationary element. So the amounts are expressed in 1965 £s or 1980 £s through all years.

Contango

Once a stock market term for deferring settlement, but that usage has been eliminated by rolling settlement. The term survives in futures trading as an alternative to forwardation (qv).

Convertibility

The ability to change the currency of one country into those of others. With legal limitations and investment premiums in some countries, the degree of convertibility varies but it is becoming more fashionable to allow the market to look after that. Many poorer countries cannot allow conversion for fear their citizens would sell all domestic cash for scarce hard currencies and so further weaken the currency.

Convertibles

Paper issued by a company, commonly loan stock, with the right to convert some time in the future into ordinary or preference shares.

Cooling off period

Rules to protect investors seem preoccupied with temperature. Even if an investor has invited a life assurance salesman to sell them a policy and has therefore avoided a cold call (qv), there is a cooling off period, which allows the investor time to think it over and change their mind. Extra information is provided and confirmation of details is sent during that time.

Corset

When the government tries to restrict the amount of credit in the economy, one way is to clamp down on banks. Setting a ceiling on lending is thought to provoke arbitrage, freezing ratios to kill competition and to borrowing elsewhere, so the Bank of England has in the past resorted to the more circuitous 'corset', officially known as supplementary special deposits.

This sets a target growth for the banks' interest-bearing eligible liabilities (mainly deposit accounts on which banks pay interest) and if exceeded the Bank of England demands a penalty by taking a portion of the cash without paying interest on it. This limits the lending base (there is a fixed multiple of assets that banks may lend) so a small tightening of the corset has a large effect on overdrafts.

Cost of living index

Like most averages, the Index of Retail Prices, as it is officially called, can be misleading. It aims to show the change in cash spending by the mythical average family, which inevitably means misrepresenting the majority of people who do not conform to that average.

Goods are weighted by their importance to the standard food basket (recalculated each year – thus undermining comparability), clothes and shoes, transport, drink tobacco, fuel and light, household goods and services.

Coupon

The rate of interest on fixed-interest security is called a coupon because at the bottom there is a series of small portions which are detached and sent off to get dividend interest payments. So, by extension, the rate of interest is frequently referred to as the security's coupon.

Cover

You can be covered by all sort of things in the City, including confusion. The most obvious one in general use is insurance cover. Another popular one is dividend cover (qv).

Crash

Financial people are surprisingly mercurial and have a fondness for graphic hyperbole. So any sharp fall in the stock market index is called a crash. The most famous one and with the most unpleasant effects was the Great Crash in the autumn of 1929. The people should have realized the worsening situation when the then US President, Herbert Hoover, said in December 1929 'Conditions are fundamentally sound'. Between 3 September 1929 and 2 July 1932 the Dow Jones Industrial Average fell from 381.7 to 41.2.

According to the tendentious economist J K Galbraith, that crash was caused by social inequality (5 per cent of the people had 33 per cent of the personal income), and by inadequate structural control so fraudsters sucked huge amounts of money out of major corporations. On top of that, the banking structure meant if one fell over the others would follow like dominoes, and the US government made decisions that aggravated conditions because it did not know what was really going on.

Crawling peg

One of the solutions to the rigidities imposed by the fixed currency parities of Bretton Woods (qv) was thought to be small but frequent adjustments which would remove the strains. But brief thought showed that it made much more sense to let the currency find its own level and once the psychological barrier was breached floating became acceptable.

Credit and charge cards

Credit cards such as Visa and Mastercard normally allow a period of grace of say 25 days when no interest is charged on the outstanding debt. After that you pay off a minimum amount and pay interest on the rest.

By contrast, charge cards like American Express and Diners Club expect instant repayment, and can get pretty annoyed if the money is not handed over. The advantage therefore is that one can leave the wallet and cheque book at home. Another difference used to be the unlimited amount of spending charge cards permit, but that has been somewhat eroded by the arrival of gold and platinum charge cards.

Some shops have their own credit cards, usually charging a higher rate of interest than most Visa and Mastercard issuers. See also Debit cards.

Credit unions

A club of people who pool their savings to lend to members at rates which make no surplus profit.

Crest

A system of settling deals on the Stock Exchange electronically.

Critical illness

See Health insurance.

Cum

Schooling at one time meant a classical education and the snobbery persists even outside the law and medicine. Cum is another example, being Latin for with. It indicates shares are sold cum cap, cum div, or cum rights, meaning that the buyer acquires entitlement to an imminent capitalization issue (also known as scrip (qv)), dividend, or rights issue. The opposite is xd, (qv) etc.

Current ratio

The current liabilities of a business related to its current assets, which is a good, quick guide to the state of its finances and whether it is solvent. You cannot compare the ratios between different industries however because industries have widely differing terms of trade.

Current assets comprise cash, bank deposits and anything else than can be turned into cash almost instantly. Current liabilities include borrowings for under a year and trade credit.

Cycles

This is about trade, not transport.

There is a tide in human affairs, and though the ebbs are clearly visible on graph paper nobody has yet managed to stop the economic fluctuations. Many analyses have shown when these cycles occurred. Between 1792 and 1913 there were 15 cycles in Britain (an eight-year average, against six to ten for Europe and three to five in the United States). Then came World War I and its consequent upturn, the long inter-war slump, which pushed British unemployment to over 20 per cent, and the upturn in the preparations for World War II.

After the war came a 28-year upsurge, which was unprecedented in size, but fluctuations on a smaller scale persisted with downturns in 1957–8, 1960–2, 1965–6, 1969–70, 1980–5 and 1990–1993. Such four- to five-year cycles were reckoned to be superimposed on a longer cycle of slightly over 10-year periods, which was suggested in the 19th century as well when the economist William Stanley Jevons linked it to the 11-year sunspot cycles.

For the world as a whole, even longer super-cycles of 45 to 60 years (but averaging 54 years) were set out in 1922 by the Russian Nikolai Kondratieff, who died in Stalin's prisons for his pains. He found the big swings were 1790s–1840s, 1840s–1890s, 1890s–1930s. To put it another way, troughs occurred in the early 1800s, 1840s, 1890s, and 1930s – which suggested a down phase in the late 1980s or early 1990s, some 50 years after the Great Depression. Kondratieff said the first sign is agricultural depression.

Another version is the Elliott Wave Theory (developed in the 1930s), which found the stock market moving in repeated patterns: each upswing is characterized by three upwaves and two down (and each downward trend shows two down and one up). The final fifth up-wave of the cycle from 1932 began in August 1982 and peaked in late 1988 as predicted.

Joseph Schumpeter ascribed such swings to technological innovation displacing traditional goods, Jay Forrester blamed them on the rise and fall of capital investment, and some attribute them to the accumulation and destruction of debt. Even short-term cycles are by definition regular and hence predictable, yet British industrialists invest at the peak and fail to invest in the trough, which leaves them financially vulnerable on the downturn and short of capacity during recovery. As a result, Britain has a diminishing share of world trade and at upturns suffers trade deficits as imports fill the gap.

In Japan it is different. During the 1986 problems, for instance, caused by the strength of the yen, falling profits and turnover prompted industrialists there to big increases in research and capital spending (eg Konishiroku, which raised both by over 20 per cent).

Dawn raid

A sudden spurt of share buying in a specific company, usually to build up a stake for a take-over bid. It takes place at the Stock Exchange's idea of dawn, about 8.30 am, with the raider being allowed to buy up to 14.9 per cent of the target shares (the maximum allowed by the Take-Over Panel rules) in one fell swoop before the price has time to rise against them.

Dead-cat bounce

A small short-term recovery in a falling stock market. A rather sick metaphor: even a dead cat will bounce slightly if dropped from high enough, but that does not mean it has come back to life.

Debenture

Companies raise money from a variety of sources and success is balancing them right for minimum cost and maximum flexibility. They can issue shares or they can borrow. Long-term borrowing secured as mortgage on the company's fixed assets with a specified rate of interest is called a debenture.

It sometimes has a repayment date at par (face value), and comes ahead of ordinary shares for payment of interest. Debentures do not benefit from higher profits so the price does not move with the company's fortunes but fluctuates with interest rates to produce comparable yields (the yield is slightly lower than on preference shares).

Debit cards

Unlike either credit or charge cards (qv), these really are just an alternative to writing a cheque or handing over cash. The shop swipes the card – like a Switch or Vector – through a terminal and if there is enough cash in the account the money is transferred. It lacks the charm of cheques therefore, which have to be paid in to a bank, cleared and debited from the customer's account. That can take four days even if everyone acts with normal promptness. Most debit cards have a secondary life for traditionalists by acting as a cheque guarantee card.

Deed of variation

A legal document altering the terms of a will after its author has died. For example the amounts allocated to beneficiaries or the people inheriting can be altered, but only with the agreement of anyone standing to benefit.

Defined benefits scheme

An alternative name for final salary pension schemes (qv).

Defined contributions scheme

Another label for the money purchase type of pension (qv).

Deflation

When the economy of a country overheats because there is more cash than goods, prices are forced up and non-monetarist governments try to reduce inflation by deflating. The usual way is to reduce demand to eliminate the original imbalance. But that can cause recession, leaving inflation rampant, especially if unions continue to demand accelerating pay rises while short-time working pushes up unit costs. The monetarist argument is that inflation is caused not by costs but purely by excess cash in the economy. Deflation will work if prices rise from too much demand, but is nasty medicine for industry. And if the real culprit is rising raw material costs, or wages rising faster than productivity, it is not just painful but wrong. In theory, inflation caused by unjustified pay rises could be countered by incomes policies but that has proved at best a short-term palliative. If the cause is soaring material costs, the country can try upvaluing its currency. If the problem is too fast an increase in money supply, the government can try controlling the portion under its control. Unfortunately for economists (and the rest of us), causes are not so neatly attributable and cures are either extremely painful or ineffective.

Deflationary gap

If people do not spend enough to keep the country at full production, the spare capacity is called the deflationary gap. One solution is to allow the economy to slip back until spending equals production and then start back up from this equilibrium, but it is painful. Another is for industry to invest in plant to create extra work and hence extra income, but companies do not have the money and lack the courage to invest in a declining economy.

The third solution, proposed by Lord Keynes (qv), is for government to fill the gap by its own expenditure funded by borrowing. But circumstances have changed in the 50 years since his proposal – government spending leads to inflation, which increases saving and frightens industry out of any investment. The problem therefore gets worse and unemployment rises. Economists are still wrestling with the dilemma.

Deposit account

Most financial institutions such as banks and building societies offer a current account with money flowing in and out continuously and often with a cheque book; and a deposit account where interest (or higher interest) is paid on the balance, but withdrawals need notice or are more difficult.

But competition has made the situation so complicated that it is not just customers who do not know what is available – even at their own bank or building society – but the institutions themselves have got tangled in their own marketing. As a result customers have been left in accounts no longer on offer because better terms are offered to tempt new depositors, and they have not been told that they could do better by shifting to the latest scheme.

In general, the longer you commit to leaving the money untouched (say one, three or six months) the higher the interest, and in most cases there is also a sliding scale with the rates improving as the amount on deposit increases. The terms and account names change so often that anybody trying to get the best rates could be shifting money on a weekly basis.

Deposit protection scheme

Depositors in banks that go bust get back 90 per cent of the first £20,000 of their money thanks to the fund set up by the Banking Act of 1987.

Depreciation

The steady shrinking of the pound in everyone's pocket caused by inflation is domestic depreciation. The currency of countries with high domestic inflation and balance of payments problems declines against other currencies and this is international depreciation.

Derivatives

A set of financial instruments derived from, or based on, normal everyday assets such as shares or money. So some examples are futures contracts, warrants, options and swaps. Clearly the value of these instruments will depend on the price of the underlying asset plus an expectation of market trends. Derivatives can thus be used to hedge (qv) a trader's dangerously exposed position, or to gamble on market movements. As the market is traded on only a small deposit, huge gearings can be achieved ensuring enormous profits and catastrophic losses, as Barings and Daiwa banks discovered.

Devaluation

A reduction in the value of a currency in terms of others is a devaluation. It is usually measured against the dollar or a basket of currencies of the major trading nations. The opposite movement, when a currency moves up against the rest is, for some obscure reason, known as revaluation.

Developing countries

Yet another euphemism for nations stuck in chronic poverty.

Direct debit

This is similar to spreading your wallet on the table and saying, help yourself as seems appropriate. The system sets up an arrangement for the recipient of regular payments, such as for mortgage, credit card, phone, electricity and council tax, to take the money out of the account on a due date. When interest rates rise or the bill increases, the company decides how much to extract.

Banks have been encouraging greater use of the facility by customers and force them to agree to this arrangement by penalizing the alternative of standing orders (qv) with higher charges. They claim the cost is lower but that is unconvincing and cynics suspect the main reason is that when things go wrong (as they do) the organization extracting the money is held to blame rather than the bank. The recipients like it because even with that odium they are certain of receiving the money and the transaction is under their own control.

Dirty float

Governments and central banks intervening covertly to manipulate the international value of their currencies while pretending to be permitting a free market float are thought to be playing dirty. Most do it when convenient.

Discount

The Stock Exchange can be confusing when it uses a common word in a specialist sense, and bewildering when the same word has several different meanings. Shares are at a discount when the price is lower than the one at which they were offered to the public. It can also be the margin by which a share stands below its par value (face value).

As a verb, however, the market is said to discount a future event when the present value of the share already allows for it. So a high price may discount an anticipated profit rise, and a low price may discount the effect of a predicted supplier strike. As a result, when the developments are made public the share price may not move at all or may even move in a paradoxical way if the events were not precisely in line with expectations: eg a profits fall was not as had been feared or was now thought to be out of the way and the market is discounting the next results; and of course vice versa.

In finance discounting is the method of calculating the present value of money to be received in the future. Discounted cash flow works on the assumption that cash now is worth more than later because inflation reduces value and because money in hand could be earning interest.

Discount houses

The last remnants of the cartoon financiers in top hats used to be the representatives of discount houses on their way to and from the Bank of England. Their work of shifting short-term cash around the City has all but disappeared and the proud old names have either been submerged or absorbed into large financial institutions.

Discount houses were unique to London – elsewhere their work is done by banks. The Radcliffe Committee summed it up well in 1959: 'It would not be beyond human ingenuity to replace the work of discount houses, but they are there, they are doing the work effectively, and they are doing it at a trifling cost in terms of labour and other real resources.' Despite that, their day is passing or has passed.

Discount rate

In theory, this is a general term for the rate of interest at which national central banks lend to commercial banks and other financial institutions, and was used in Britain for the Bank of England's way of setting national interest rates before it was replaced by bank rate, minimum lending rate and other such euphemisms. In the United States it is still used for the rate charged by the Federal Reserve Board to banks which borrow from it.

Discounted cash flow

See Cash flow.

Disinflation

Economists trying to explain inflation confuse the layman by coining words that sound distressingly similar, so we have inflation, hyperinflation, stagflation, reflation, deflation, and disinflation. Unhappily, the proliferation of labels has not been paralleled by a similar growth in understanding causes or in evolving cures.

Disinflation is what the authorities are aiming for – slowing down the rate of price rises – while deflation (in the sense of cutting demand) is one of the methods they use. There are other ways, and which one is used should depend on what caused the inflation. If inflation is imported through higher raw material costs, raising the value of the currency helps through making imports cheaper. But this works only for a strong economy with spare manufacturing capacity (cheapening imports boosts demand) and often involves higher interest rates, which are unpopular. The policy is tricky: it is just as bad to fall flat on one's back as to fall on one's face. Revaluation is clearly out of the question for countries with currencies under pressure, or high domestic inflation as well, but unfortunately that is often the case.

Other methods of disinflation include prices and incomes policy. But pay control is seldom achieved and never effective long (see Incomes policy); and suppressing prices starves manufacturers of profits needed for investment. Governments can keep down the cost of living by subsidies, but even that cash has to come from somewhere (the taxpayer) and the long-term effects can be dire.

Disintermediation

When governments try to restrict the growth of money supply or of borrowing, the handiest weapon is a clamp-down on bank lending. As borrowers still need cash, they merely go elsewhere for it and the obvious place is institutions and companies with spare capital.

Since the parties no longer use an intermediary, this is

disintermediation and as the transaction does not appear in official statistics the government's figures look to have attained the objectives until restrictions are removed. Then the loans are renegotiated through banks – reintermediated – and the official statistics go haywire.

Dividend cover

Dividend cover is the number of times a company's available profits cover the money needed to pay dividends. It gives an idea of how much spare cash flow the company has and therefore how safe the dividend is.

Dividend yield

See Yield.

Domestic credit expansion

One of a long series of vain attempts to trap volatile money supply in tightly defined and hence measurable categories, in the hope that what can be defined can be controlled.

In an open economy like the UK, the external sector, like the balance of trade and money markets, can swamp domestic controls of money supply. Domestic credit expansion was thought to be an answer. It is defined as notes and coins in circulation, plus UK banks' loans at home and overseas and overseas loans to the British public sector (see also Money supply).

Domestic fixed capital formation

Durable fixed assets – such as cars and lorries, new buildings, machinery and equipment – whether bought as addition to existing stock or to replace worn out equivalents, but maintenance and repair are excluded.

Domicile

An important word in tax, which sounds pretty much the same as residence, but is not. Domicile is not determined by either residence or nationality but in effect what a person is ultimately reckoned to call home. The father's residence is domicile of origin. A person leaving to live elsewhere acquires a domicile of choice, but if they become so rootless no choice is obvious, and the domicile of origin reactivates.

Double-taxation agreement

Fearsome though this sounds, it is actually the opposite of what it says: an arrangement between countries to prevent the same money being taxed twice. They are bilateral treaties, which for example, say that income generated in one country but received in another is not hot in both.

Dow Jones

The index showing trends in the New York Stock Exchange. Like the FT Industrial Ordinary Index in Britain, it is calculated from price movements of 30 representative large companies, but without the mathematical complexity of the UK calculation – ie in New York they add the 30 prices and adjust them by a 'current average divisor' while the FT Index (qv) requires a lot more mathematics. The base year for the main index is 1928, and there are specialist group indices as well for transport, utilities and bonds. It was started in 1884 by the financial news service founded by Charles H Dow and Edward D Jones in 1882. Originally, they had a messenger service for delivering slips to finance houses but the last delivery each day added a news summary, which eventually grew to be the *Wall Street Journal*, which Dow edited. He also evolved a theory for share price prediction (see Charts).

Dow theory

One of the fundamental theories or charts (qv) laid down by Charles H Dow. It says that the market is on an upward trend if the industrial or transport index reaches a new high followed by a similar peak in the other. Conversely, if they successively dip to new lows that is confirmation of a downward trend.

Drop lock

A loan with interest rate floating in parallel with some managed rate but, if it drops to an agreed level, it is locked there for the remainder of the loan term.

Due diligence

Of course professionals should be exercising due diligence throughout their work, but the only time it is explicitly mentioned is when they start investigating the finances of a company when it becomes the target of a take-over agreement. Then the bidder sends in the accountants to investigate what the outfit is really worth. It is when the investigators fail to spot fraud, mistakes and incompetence and the purchase turns out to be worthless that the big litigations start.

Dumping

A highly emotional subject in international trade – it is defined as selling overseas at lower prices than in the home market, or as selling abroad at less than the cost of production plus selling cost and a reasonable profit. Countries often accuse each other of this and wild accusations emerge from trade associations, but dumping is very hard to prove. Countries have muttered darkly about Japanese overseas selling tactics but have found the flexible price lists and complex deals in the domestic market-makes it impossible to establish home selling prices.

Some states get round the problem by analysing the nearest equivalent home producer's costs and if the imports are inexplicably cheaper they assume dumping until proved otherwise. Britain requires direct proof and so seldom takes anti-dumping action despite heart-rending pleas from home producers.

International agreement allows that proved dumping can be fought by a duty to cancel the price advantage and so prevent damage to domestic manufacturers. It makes sense since the overseas company, having bankrupted native suppliers (assuming its own finances can take the strain any longer) has the monopoly with corresponding freedom over price and supply.

Dutch auction

A much misused expression. It is the reverse of the normal auction in which each bidder tries to top his rivals. In a Dutch auction the auctioneer starts with a high price and gradually reduces it until a buyer is found. It is a poker-like battle of nerves, with the first to crack buying the goods.

Earnings yield

See Yield.

Easdaq

One of the problems with European stock markets is their concentration on old, large companies misses the excitement of dynamic young innovators which might tempt in the private investors. That and risk-aversion have meant that hardly any British shares are held by private investors.

France, Germany and Britain have started separate markets for young companies, and Easdaq has is trying to replicate the success, in the United States, of Nasdaq (qv), on which it is modelled. It is a Europe-wide electronic market but the high cost of joining and stiff entry qualifications have so far kept away the crowds.

Econometric forecasting

Like getting married for the second time, this demonstrates the victory of hope over experience. It also shows faith that computers will succeed where centuries of thought and prayer have failed: foretelling the future. Econometrics translates business relationships and financial activity into mathematical formulae but humans still work out the ratios and program assumptions. So the prize has proved even more elusive than reliable weather forecasting. One can extrapolate (qv) existing trends, assuming stability, or predict how relationships will change, and then make human guesses about how and when. Nevertheless, government, stockbrokers, universities and specialist professionals by the dozens continue trying. The better ones are within a percent or two for most factors, but even that small an error can make such huge differences that policies would have to be altered, and on some figures like the balance of payments (the difference between two large sums) errors are wide. Computers have improved accuracy little and the effort proves the old adage about the difficulty in prediction, especially of the future.

Economies of scale

The notion that if one makes more of something then the price of each individual item will be lower. A fine 18th-century theory which applied well to 18th-century production and where the same overheads are spread over more products. In pursuit of this elusive ideal, many British companies were shotgunned into marriages in the belief that if they grew as big as US, Japanese and European rivals, they would be as efficient. Rover (formerly British Motor Holdings, British Leyland, BLMC, Austin-Morris, as it tried hide behind regular name changes) is a good example of this fallacy: when created it had some 42 per cent of the British car market, but over subsequent years that dropped to about 10 per cent. The rule about amalgamations is that merging an efficient company with an inefficient one produces a large inefficient company.

Reaction to these unwieldy industrial monsters was led by Schumacher in his book, *Small is Beautiful*. Efficiency of production was often more than offset by strains in managing enormous units, and usefully creative people disliked working for large organizations. So there is a trend to local control, and management buy-outs of subsidiaries have become increasingly popular.

Ecu

European Union budgets and contributions were calculated in European Currency Units (with the acronym pronounced as if it were a French word) defined in terms of member currencies. It was created to be the foundation for the integrated European Monetary System.

But for the European monetary union a new currency was invented with the bland compromise name of euro.

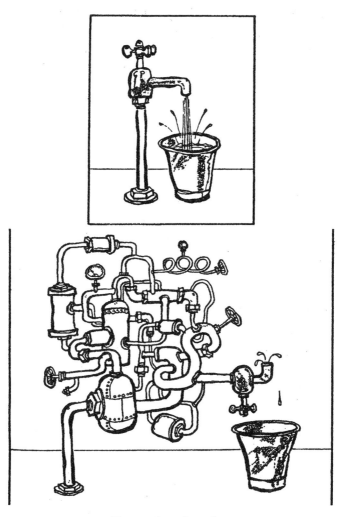

Economies of scale

Eftpos

It is easier to cope with the contraction than the full name, electronic fund transfer at point of sale. It just means the terminal in a shop, which accepts a debit card (qv) so the cost of the goods is debited to the customer's account and transferred to the shopkeeper's.

Egibi

The oldest recorded bank. During the time of the Babylonian king Sennacherib in the seventh century BC Mr Egibi ran a banking operation in Damascus and a record of one his loans is on a stone tablet now in the British Museum.

Elasticity

Another example of economists taking a normal word and making it mean something quite different. To money people, price elasticity of demand measures how much sales move in response to a change in price. If sales change proportionately more than the price, demand is called elastic; if less, inelastic.

So the actual degree of elasticity is percentage change of sales divided by percentage change of price. The demand for cigarettes, for example, is inelastic, within reason, because a 10 per cent rise in price causes only a minimal reduction in smoking.

There is a similar form of measure of demand related to changes in income.

Elliott wave theory

See Cycles.

Emerging markets

The label comes into the same class of euphemism/optimism as 'developing country' or 'welfare-to-work'. There are gamblers, however, who thought that stock markets in places like Istanbul, Warsaw, Manila, Caracas, Budapest, Lima and Mexico would grow faster than long-established exchanges like London, Amsterdam, New York and Tokyo. The turbulence in the Far East economies during 1997/8 and the regularly troubled finances of Latin America have cooled some of the enthusiasm. But then Tokyo itself was hardly immune. Money has been made in some of these markets but at some risk – as some very bruised investors can testify.

Emerging nations

Euphemism for profound national poverty.

Endowment

A type of life assurance which pays a specified sum on an agreed date (or death if that occurs earlier), often used in connection with mortgages even when a straight repayment system would be better, because the salesman gets a better commission.

Enterprise Investment Scheme

Yet another government effort to coax investment into small businesses without promoting blatant tax avoidance scams. It supplanted the Business Expansion Scheme and reduces income tax liability on investments up to £100 000 a year in unquoted companies, and also avoids capital gains tax on such shares held more than five years.

Equities

Companies issue a wide range of paper ranging from loan stock, through convertibles to preference shares. The most common is the ordinary share (called common stock in the United States), which is also equity.

Dividends for equities come from what is left when all else is paid, so at times of stringency payments could well stop. Similarly, holders are last in line for payment at insolvency. So the share price closely reflects the health (more usually the expected health) of the company which issues them.

Escrow

In law, a written obligation between two people who give it to a third party to hold while a specified condition is met, for example making a payment. In financial circles it usually refers to a specialized bank account holding money in dispute, to prevent either side getting their hands on it, and also to make sure any interest accrued goes to the winner. The cash is put into an independent person's account specifically held during the resolution of the argument.

Ethical investments

Actually, it is investment in 'ethical' sectors. In practice, those are defined negatively: no tobacco, armaments, alcohol, experimenting on animals or causing pollution. Some follow the course from personal conviction and some from the self-interested view that such companies will grow faster.

Euro

The boring and uninspired name, invented by a committee, for the currency used by members of the European Union which joined monetary union to use a common currency.

Eurocurrency

Despite the name, this has nothing to do with monetary union. It is actually commonly not even European in origin.

First came Eurodollars, which piled up in Europe as Americans lent and spent. It was put to work by companies which needed dollars and found extraterritorial cash convenient. Others have followed, including the Euroyen. The charm of Eurocurrencies lies in the total lack of control over them by any government but, despite that, their wide acceptability.

European Bank for Reconstruction and Development

The institution was set up to give financial help to eastern Europe, but started off on the wrong foot when it helped largely itself by building a London headquarters of spectacular lavishness. The European Union was the main instigator, the office is in the UK, but the senior staff is mainly French. Like other such attempts to help countries decolonized by Russia, a large amount of the money goes to accountants and consultants giving advice to western governments about where the money should go, and advising local businesses on how to work harder.

European currency unit

See Ecu.

European Investment Bank (EIB)

A European Union institution set up to help areas of poverty and unemployment. The EIB gets money from member states and provides grants and loans for industrial projects. For a long time distressed parts of Britain and Italy received two-thirds of the cash, with much of the rest going to signatories of the Lomé Convention.

European monetary union

The aim is for a single currency, the euro, to be used throughout the European Union. Its advocates say it works perfectly well in the US, it will eliminate the dangers and cost of moving exchange rates, and make it easier to compare prices across the whole continent.

Its opponents object that the euro will be weakened by dodgy economies being shoehorned into the system, a common currency under central control will remove controls from the finance ministries in the constituent countries, and subvention will flow even faster from the strong to the weak.

Evasion

Forget normal English usage where avoidance and evasion are interchangeable, with neither attracting more odium. Tax experts, for some obscure reason, decided that avoidance is taking permissible advantage of allowances, while evasion is the nasty, reprehensible, and illegal method of not paying tax which the law demands.

Exceptional

The point of company accounts is to show how the normal business is run, so fortuitous losses and windfall gains should be separated to prevent confusing longer-term trends. Accounting differentiates these one-off items and calls them exceptional and extraordinary (qv) items. Exceptional is shown as part of a company's pre-tax profit because, although unusually large or not expected to recur regularly, it derives from the company's normal run of business.

Exchange rate mechanism

The much-debated linkage between currencies of the EU which prevented their values drifting far from a pre-set level, except by agreement. It is sometimes supposed by the superstitious to curtail exchange rate fluctuations and inflation, though without any serious explanation of how that could happen.

Expenses

It costs money to deal in shares – unless one is a major financial institution and can afford it. Among the expenses to be calculated before a profit can be made are the broker's commission (widely variable and sometimes open to negotiation), stamp duty, and company registration fees (most companies do not charge). And the market-maker's spread – the difference between their buying and selling price – should not be forgotten.

Export Credits Guarantee Department

A government-sponsored body which insures exporters against failure to get their money. Either directly or through the bank financing the sale, it provides short-term protection against the buyer's insolvency, block on the payments by overseas government, war, cancellation of the import licence, and exchange control problems.

The body was set up in 1930 and is supposed to break even, so its premiums reflect the risk. A large chunk was sold off to a Dutch insurance business.

Extraordinary

Definitions in commerce are often arbitrary. For instance, in accounting extraordinary items are differentiated from exceptional (qv) by being 'below the line', ie after the pre-tax profit figure which is the standard measure of corporate performance.

The separation is to show that the money is outside the normal activities of the business and not generally expected to recur. Examples have been redundancy payments, sales of factories and the like. In the United States this is called 'unusual'. That sounds subjective. It is. Companies have got away with flagrant manipulation of these figures and auditors have sanctioned identical subjects being treated in totally different ways.

Extraordinary general meeting

Any meeting called for a company's shareholders other than the regular annual general meeting is deemed extraordinary. One can be called by the directors or by holders of over 10 per cent of the shares.

Extrapolation

This is the belief that the future will be much the same as the past so current trends may be extended to show what is to come. The word was coined as converse of interpolate, just as the Treasury talks of a longfall as opposed to a shortfall in government spending. Extrapolation is a distressingly common form of forecasting, either when managers do not think about their assumptions or when economists purport to do something more complicated. It is unlikely to be right, since the one lesson from the past is that economic relationships are not stable. Since even the direction and speed of change are inconsistent, forecasters have found it hard to eliminate a random element from their projections.

This is the main reason that forecasters are often wrong and economic explanations deal with the past.

Factoring

A way of collecting cash immediately on invoices, without having to wait until customers get around to it, by selling them on to a specialist company which then assumes responsibility for credit control and risk, as well as debt collection. Similar to invoice discounting but with a wider range of service.

Fan club

This is real admiration: these fans put up large amounts of money to show how much they care. The phrase in the City has come to be connected with contested take-overs or other conflicts, and applies to a group of investors (often themselves companies) which is supposed to be acting out of a disinterested appreciation of a manager's capability.

Hence they buy shares at crucial moments, or back one side with their holdings. They are not supposed to have colluded either with each other or with the admired director, but in practice it is often a 'concert party' (qv) which nobody can prove.

Fiduciary

Bank notes which promise to pay the bearer on demand £5, £10 and so on are liars – the Bank of England has reneged on these contracts for a very long time and refuses to pay over the backing value in gold. One good reason is that there is not enough gold to cover the issue of cash completely – most of the currency has no backing at all and depends on faith (fiducia is the Latin for confidence, reliance, trust) and on the fact that it is legal tender; Scottish notes rely on faith alone.

Final salary pension

Sometimes called a defined benefit pension because the amount received depends on the amount of the salary in the final years before retirement with the exact proportion dependent on the number of years' service. The other sort of money-purchase pension (qv).

Financial Services Authority

The regulatory body monitoring financial services sold to the public and enforcing the regulations brought in by the Financial Services Act. It is the latest in a regular revamping of the bodies keeping an eye on the money people.

Fiscal drag

Tax systems are 'progressive', which misleadingly suggests approbation (assuming that progress is a Good Thing), though it means only the proportion taken increases with the size of the income. During inflation the money received in pay increases (though the value may be constant) and as a result taxpayers are gradually pushed into ever higher tax brackets and the state surreptitiously takes a steadily growing portion of incomes. This is fiscal drag. To offset this, thresholds and allowances should be indexed.

Fiscal policy

The word fiscal is derived from fiscus, a Roman emperor's treasury, and deals with the policy of tax and spending and their effects on the economy. So it covers taxation, national debt, and government borrowing with consideration of the results on demand.

Fiscal year

Fiscal year

If one want to send one's tax inspector a New Year card, it should arrive on 6 April, as, with puzzling contrariness, tax authorities resolutely ignore calendars used by the rest of us. But there is a reason.

Julius Caesar introduced the Julian calendar in 46 BC. It was quite good but lost 11 minutes and 10 seconds a year, so as the error accumulated Pope Gregory shifted everything around in 1582. With splendid insularity, Henry VIII wanted none of this Continental nonsense (especially as it had been devised by a Pope). It was not until 1752 that Britain adjusted, by which time the calendar was 11 days behind. So 3 September became 14 September, provoking riots from people who resented losing 11 days from their lives. Russia, incidentally, was even more sluggish and did not change until 1918, which is why the October Revolution actually took place in November.

On moving to the Gregorian calendar the start of the civil and legal year was moved from Lady Day on 25 March to 1 January (with Scotland lagging behind until 1600). Accounting and tax, however, follow Customs, commerce and navigation, with quarter days being used. In 1800 that was 5 January but in 1832 they plumped for Lady Day. Once the 11 missing days of 1752 were added back though, 25 March became 5 April. Yes, the thing sounds wholly implausible but there we are.

The US fiscal year started on 1 October – there is a story to that too.

Five-day trading

Buyers of shares must pay up within five working days by which time the sellers have to produce the certificates. This replaced the fortnightly trading account in 1995 and is in the process of coming down to three working days.

Floating currency

After decades battling against reality, governments realized that a prevailing exchange rate had no hallowed privilege. Currencies under pressure had been forced into sacrifices as central banks (eg the Bank of England) poured out hard-earned foreign exchange in a vain attempt to stem the tide. And governments defended the currency by trade balances and so stopped the economy dead in an attempt to cut imports.

Eventually, the market was trusted to find the appropriate level. This meant abandoning the Smithsonian Agreement (qv) as well as Bretton Woods (qv), but at least removed stigma from devaluation (qv) and allowed governments to use exchange rates as another tool for managing the economy.

The first major currency to take the plunge was Canada in 1950. Many governments planned to return to fixed rates and from time to time still hanker for that predictability. They also still intervene, either individually or more usually with the other major economies, to reduce the volatility of swings.

Flotation

The coming of a company to the stock market. It is floated when its shares start to be quoted. When it sinks they are not.

FOB/CIF

Overseas trade is normally priced as free on board (FOB), which means the exporter pays to get the goods to the ship's hold, or carriage insurance and freight (CIF), which means the seller pays for transport and insurance to destination, or just cost and freight. Britain's exports used to be counted FOB and imports CIF, which had the logic of dealing with goods at the point they cross the coast, but the figures got confusing. Statistics now count FOB values and separate the rest into invisibles (qv).

Forfaiting

One of the specialist financing techniques used by companies to collect their cash quickly rather than wait for the customer to get round to paying their bills. It is mainly used by exporters of expensive engineering items, like the discounting of bills of exchange and promissory notes. But in forfaiting they are guaranteed by a bank in the buyer's home country, so the exporter is not liable even if the overseas company goes under.

Forward market

In currencies, commodities and securities one can deal for immediate delivery (spot market) or to get the goods some time in the future at a price agreed now (forward market). Clearly, the two can be balanced and played off against each other, not just for speculation but as a safety measure for users of the commodity etc. A chocolate maker, for instance, might limit cost rises over a period through forward deals. This is part of the intriguingly science-fiction title of the futures market.

Forwardation

If commodities are cheaper on the spot market (for immediate delivery) than on the forward market (for later delivery), a dealer can buy now for their future obligations. Such an unusual relation of prices is called forwardation.

Franchise

A neat way to make money without doing the heavy work is telling others how to do it. If one has a big new consumer idea – a new type of fast food, a quick way to unblock drains, a printing facility, or replacing tyres quickly – one registers and publicizes the scheme and gets small investors to operate the system in their own area in return for a royalty payment. The central organizer provides design, costings, supplies materials, and manages advertising.

Franked income

Income which has already paid corporation tax. Funds have to differentiate to ensure they do not pay again.

Free-standing

See Additional voluntary contributions.

Frictional unemployment

Lack of knowledge by employers that workers are available and by workers of what jobs are going means there are unemployed in one area and unfilled jobs in another. Advertising reduces the problem but the difficulties of moving and the cost of property reduces labour mobility and so increases frictional unemployment.

Friendly society

Sounds cosy. In a way rightly so, because such organizations were set up to help members rather than make a profit. The origins go back to at least the 16th century, when they operated from a local inn to help poor and sick members, their widows and orphans, in return for regular contributions. They spread to became a more generalized way of saving or insurance for sickness, burial, medical expenses, or life. Some divide surpluses among members. Since 1846 they have been supervised by the Chief Registrar of Friendly Societies who gets an annual return and audits the books. In addition to the original organizations, the label covers co-operatives, trade unions and building societies.

Front end loading

The two different uses of this phrase have much the same implication: cash up front. Repayment of loans such as mortgages or hire purchase contracts includes both interest and capital. The normally level repayments throughout the term of the contract (unless interest changes) are at the beginning nearly all interest, with very little capital content. This is one sense. As the loan nears the end, the interest element declines and the capital content rises until towards the end it is nearly all capital.

When one buys unit trusts, life assurance or a pension contract, the buying costs are loaded onto the initial payments. As a result, the first payment is often nearly all commission with negligible investment – the costs of entering the scheme are contained in the initial payment or premium. This is another meaning of front end loading and an explanation of why cashing in a policy at the start yields such a small return.

Front running

A stock market scam. Brokers and market-makers sometimes get advance warning of a big deal or of information about to be circulated to institutions, either of which will move the share price appreciably. If they can get in for a quiet piece of personal trading there is a rapid but illicit profit.

FT Index

Trying to judge share price trends by adding together individual price changes would produce misleading results. In some companies hardly any shares are available for trade so a few deals can cause wide price swings; small companies attract speculative buying; and cheap shares costing a few pence are more liable to large percentage moves. So indices have been evolved to give a true picture of the market. In Britain the most commonly used one for a long time has been the Financial Times Ordinary Share Index, usually called the FT Index, which consists of 30 large companies across a broad range of industries and with actively traded shares. It was started at 100 in 1935. Since then insolvency, take-overs and economic upheavals have replaced practically all the original companies.

The index is the geometric mean of the prices, divided by the price at the base date. For the mathematically minded, this is done by adding the logarithms of the share values, deducting the base value, dividing by 30, and then taking the antilog of the result.

A wider version, the FT-SE 100 Index (abbreviated to Footsie), covering, as its name implies, 100 leading companies, was started at the start of 1984 at 1000 and, like the Standard and Poor's 100 Index in the United States is a weighted arithmetic index. In addition there are industry sector indices and the FT All Share Index, which, contrary to its name, covers 500 shares.

All stock markets have some index: the United States has The Dow Jones as well as the Standard and Poor's; Hong Kong has the Hang Seng; Singapore the Fraser's and the Straits Times indices; Tokyo has Nikkei; and so on.

Fundamental analysis

Trying to discover the value of a company, and hence its shares, by analysing its financial performance and prospects, as opposed to chartist analysis, which looks at only the share price.

Funds

Another name for British government stocks, but rarely used now (see Gilt-edged).

Fungible

Anything equivalent, replaceable, interchangeable. So, for instance, every £10 note is exchangeable for every other and futures contracts in the same commodity and same delivery month and meeting standard specifications of equal quantity etc are fungible. Securities in a clearing system which are not allocated to owners by serial numbers are also fungible, as are bearer instruments.

Futures Market

See Forward market.

G

GATT

See World Trade Organization.

Gazumping

Gentlemen's agreements do not stand up well to the pressure of money. If one has agreed to sell one's house but goes back on the deal when a better offer comes along, the first buyer has been gazumped. If there is no contract and no cash paid, he has no legal recourse but an oral agreement has been repudiated.

It has always seemed immoral, especially when the first buyer could lose substantial sums in solicitors' and surveyors' fees, but it is common when property prices boom. It is not permissible in Scotland.

Gearing

The ratio of a company's borrowings (overdraft plus debentures and preference shares) to ordinary shares is called gearing. A company with a high proportion of those prior charges before ordinary shares reach the head of the queue for payment, is called highly geared. Loans have to be serviced first, so at times of low profits shareholders can get little or nothing if a company is heavily borrowed.

In the United States it is called leverage.

General Agreement on Tariffs and Trade (GATT)

See World Trade Organization.

Gilt-edged

At the end of the 19th century the phrase gilt-edged became a popular name for the most reliable securities, including stocks issued by British and colonial governments, and debentures and shares in first-rate British companies. Now the term is generally restricted to British government securities.

Most gilts are redeemed (bought back) at face value between specified dates which can be up to 40 years away. For convenience the list is broken down into three: less than five years to redemption are called short-dated or just shorts, lives of 5 to 15 years are medium-dated, and those with over 15 years to go are long-dated or just longs. Yield varies with price, which in turn is principally set by prevailing or expected interest rates. In the newspapers gilts are quoted with dividend yield (face or par value divided by price, times nominal interest rate) and redemption yield, which includes the bonus paid by government when it redeems the stock at par.

The amount on issue depends on government borrowing needs and monetary policy. Not to be confused with Treasury Bills (qv).

Gini coefficient

Nothing to do with lightness of brown hair coming out of bottles. Popularized by the Diamond Commission before its demise in 1979, this is a measure of inequality in the distribution of income or wealth.

Simplest in graphs: along the bottom axis is plotted the population percentage, and up the vertical the percentage of wealth owned. So with complete equality 25 per cent own

25 per cent, 50 per cent own 50 per cent and so on, the result is a straight line at 45 degrees. But since this never applies (in Britain the richest 5 per cent own almost half the wealth) the line bulges away from the diagonal and the area between the two indicates the degree of inequality.

Few countries have adequate statistics to judge, and they are usually not comparable.

Giro

The Post Office Savings Bank until privatization. Not to be confused with the giro system of clearance operated by the major banks – that is just a way for passing cash among themselves across a computer network.

GNP and GDP

There is a surprisingly wide variety of ways to measure the output of an economy, and funnily enough they produce differing results.

One way is to take the national product, which includes all a country's output of goods and services, plus net property income from overseas. Leave out the property income and it becomes, reasonably enough, domestic product. If they are given gross, depreciation has not been deducted.

Both are usually taken at 'market prices' but if indirect taxes such as VAT are left out and government subsidies are added in, the result is at 'factor cost'. The results are not dependable pictures of an economy. For instance, most items are at price except public services (at cost), the self-employed ('imputed', which is a euphemism for guessed), and do-it-yourself and housewives (both ignored).

As everything sold is bought, national product equals national expenditure, and all the money goes to somebody, so they both equal national income. The logic of that is incontrovertible, so it is a little distressing that the three results are never quite the same.

Gnomes

Swiss bankers are traditionally regarded as people of independent rapacity answerable to no national government. So currency speculation, and hence wild swings in exchange rates, were attributed to machinations by the gnomes of Zurich.

As world share and currency markets have evolved, the real reason for a decline is seen to be mistrust of a government's prudence and determination. No satisfactory alternative culprit has yet been found to the gnomes, so administrations are driven to fulminations about irresponsibility and hysteria in world markets.

Gold

We are scornful of primitive tribes using cowrie shells or cocoa as currency, yet we still rely to an astonishing extent on a metal of little practical use save that, being inert, it will not corrode. It is curious how tenaciously gold has persisted as a store of value, continuing as mattress stuffing at times of uncertainty, to the exclusion of most other such goods.

It is still an important backing for national economies – reserves are held in gold and foreign exchange. Attempts to undermine its strength by creating alternatives such as 'paper gold' (special drawing rights) have been at best only partly successful. At one time Fort Knox had to hold open days to reassure people the yellow bars were still there. Buying gold diverts savings from useful industrial investment to an unproductive pile for a Scrooge. The answer may be to return to the renaissance usage of depositing gold in vaults and using the receipts as currency.

Golden handcuffs

When City specialists barely out of their teens get more money than the Prime Minister they must be awfully valuable, so their employers try very hard to keep them. Knowing the weakness for money of these (and of course other) highly-paid executives, employers shackle them to the company with a series of benefits, including share options which materialize over a protracted period.

Golden handshake

A nice farewell to a departing employee, such as a retiring director, in the form of cash or other presents, ranging from a house to an insurance policy.

Golden hello

A wily method of breaking golden handcuffs (qv) – to induce executives to leave existing employers they are tempted by filling their pockets with tenners and shares.

Golden parachute

Directors who run companies too ineptly to resist a take-over bid are keen to look after themselves better than shareholders. This is done by arranging for substantial cash payments to the board if the company changes hands. Shareholders would be wise to resist such contracts.

Goodheart's Law

Coined by Charles Goodheart, Chief Monetary Adviser to the Bank of England. For Goodheart's First Law, see Monetarist; for Goodheart's Second Law, see Money supply.

Granny bonds

The common name for index-linked National Savings certificates because when introduced in 1975 they were restricted to people over retirement age. Since then anyone can buy up to £10 000, but the attraction is greatest at times of high inflation.

Green pound

The rate of exchange between sterling and the Common Market unit of account (UA) used for pricing agricultural policy. Although the UA is allowed to float green currencies are readjusted only intermittently, after inter-governmental haggling. So normal exchange rates and green currencies can drift apart while governments decide where the balance of advantage lies – consumers want a strong green pound to keep food prices down, and farmers want the opposite.

With each country calculating similar priorities, elaborate horse trading goes on at the EU before adjustment. The system is obviously ramshackle and makeshift but the EU maintains that it works in practice.

Greenmail

Unlike blackmail, greenmail takes place over greenbacks only – that is, the whole elaborate deal is financial. The usual ploy is for a well-known predator to buy a substantial stake in a large company with the threat of launching a full bid. Since directors will always protect their existing jobs, especially in the United States, to the exclusion of almost every other consideration, they will always try to fend off a take-over. One way is to buy the predator's shares from them with the company's money, at a comfortable profit to them.

Gresham's Law

Sir Thomas Gresham, founder of the Royal Exchange in London and financial councillor to Queen Elizabeth I, is credited with a theory that good things founder while mediocrity thrives. Actually, he said something more specialized, and the theory had already been propounded in 14th-century France by Oresme, a minister of Charles V.

The law says that bad money drives out good. By this Gresham meant only that if there are two types of coin in circulation, one of which has greater inherent value, people will spend the inferior one and hoard the good one.

It happened in Britain. 'Silver' coinage was just that until 1919, made of 92 per cent real silver. Then it was de-graded, with the coins containing only half silver until 1946, after which they were of cupro-nickel. People got to hear that the silver content of the old coins was higher than the face value and hung on to them. So the good silver coin was driven out of circulation by the bad cupro-nickel. Eventually, the silver coins were demonetised – declared to be no longer legal tender – but by a special rule continued the interdiction against defacing the queen's coinage. So it is still illegal to melt them down and some people have actually been prosecuted. Gold and silver are the heart of Gresham's Law and the debasement of the coinage is usually involved.

Gross domestic product, gross national product

See GNP, GDP.

Group of Seven

See Group of Ten.

Group of Ten

Conferences are good excuses for a party and for making people feel important, so forums for economists, central bankers, finance ministers and the like continue to proliferate. There is the International Monetary Fund, the World Bank, Group of Seven, Group of Ten, Group of Twenty, World Trade Organization, Organization for Economic Cooperation and Development, Bank for International Settlements. G10, as it is sometimes called, is a club of finance ministers and top treasury officials from the ten richest non-communist countries who meet as the need arises. There are no staff and no routines, so the group tends to be more responsive to what is happening than other organizations. Another factor in its favour is its readiness to take action, such as organizing support for a country. Britain has benefited from this policy. Members are the United States, Germany, France, Italy, Netherlands, Belgium, Sweden, Canada, Japan and Britain.

Growth stock

Shares of companies expected to do really well and so make their shareholders rich through rapid increase in size (especially of profits) are called growth stocks. Although the assumption is often that this will provide capital gain, the price is generally already high and the yield therefore low because others have also had the same view. Fast growth is expected to offset this initial disadvantage.

Hammered

A stockbroker going bust is sometimes still said to be hammered, not because clients hit them but from a piece of market tradition. When a broker defaulted on debts, a waiter (a market attendant, so called from the exchange's coffee house origins) walked into the market, solemnly mounted a rostrum, hammered three times on its edge and in ringing tones announced the name of the defaulter. It does not quite work across the circuits of a computer. The exchange maintains a fund to protect investors from losses as a result of a broker becoming insolvent.

Health insurance

It is rare for the insurance industry to be as brutally frank as to call a policy a 'dread disease' insurance, especially when it talks about 'permanent health insurance' when it means permanent illness. Actually the permanent part only means that once the insurance company has accepted a customer for this type of policy it cannot later load the premiums or refuse further cover just because the policyholder has had the gall to make a claim.

Critical illness and dread disease policies pay a lump sum if the insured gets struck down by a stroke, a coronary crisis or the need for a major transplant, etc. Permanent health policies pay a regular income in case of illness or disability.

Another variant is the medical costs insurance, which provides health care as an alternative to the National Health Service.

Hedge

Sometimes the world of investments inadvertently lets slip the pompous mask of respectability and shows the true nature of the business. To hedge is a betting term, in use since the 17th century, for protecting oneself against loss on a bet by making cross-bets the other way.

In a similar way, the term now describes the way investors protect themselves against a change in value which could hurt. So one can hedge against inflation by acquiring things that will retain their real value, or buy commodities in futures markets as a hedge against current valuations, or one may buy currency forward to protect payments that have to be made in the future.

Home income plan

A scheme to provide income for elderly people. Those over 65 can take out a mortgage on the home, which by that time is probably otherwise mortgage-free, and use the money to buy an annuity. Part of the income from that pays the mortgage interest and the loan itself is repaid from the eventual sale of the property.

Hyperinflation

Economists agree this means very rapid inflation but not on where the hyper bit starts. Probably something over 20 per cent is an indication that price rises have become self-feeding and so not controllable by normal means. As numbers accelerate money ceases to have any serious purpose and only constant overprinting with ever more zeroes keeps notes in circulation at all.

That is what happened in Germany during the 1920s and in Hungary after World War II. Hungary holds the world speed record, with the period between August 1945 and July 1946. It was forced to issue first the milpengo (1 000 000 or 10^6 pengo), then the bilpengo (10^{12} pengo), then the tax pengo, which went into astronomic index numbers. The authorities finally stabilized a new unit, called the forint, at the rate of one forint equalling 4×10^{29} pengo (which is 4 followed by 29 noughts). Despite lorryfuls of notes issued by the Hungarian National Bank, people lost all faith in currency and reverted to barter, using soap, chocolates and cigarettes as currency.

No economy can survive this sort of thing unscathed. Industry cannot sensibly continue and savings cease to have value. Disruptions spread to political stability and theory has it that anything over 20 per cent undermines democracy, though Britain reached 27 per cent briefly without rioting in the streets.

Hyperinflation

Incomes policy

Recorded attempts to control wages and prices date back some 3 700 years to the Code of Hammurabi (BC 1711-1669). A later attempt was Diocletian's Edict of AD 301, typical of most such efforts in trying to treat symptoms of economic mismanagement because the alternative of attacking the real cause is uncomfortable (it causes deflation and unemployment) and is more difficult and protracted. Such Canute-like attempts have been made in most countries at some time; since World War II Austria, Norway, Canada, Australia, the United States, Netherlands and Finland have been among countries trying this palliative to stem a wages flood.

In Britain the first pay restraint was probably the Statute of Labourers of 1350, which tried to peg pay at the level of three years before. But, typically, in 1352 Parliament found employers paying double or treble, so stocks were set up in every town. When that failed, the penalties were stepped up but, like the death penalty imposed by Diocletian for transgressing his Edict, they failed.

Attempts have nevertheless recurred. After World War II there was Sir Stafford Cripps's voluntary restraint from 1948, but that lasted less than a year. In 1956 the government made pathetic pleas for pay restraint and was ignored. Selwyn Lloyd attempted a voluntary 'pay pause' in 1961 but that collapsed almost immediately. It was followed by the 2 per cent to $2\frac{1}{2}$ per cent 'guiding light', raised to $3\frac{1}{2}$ per cent in 1963 and supervised by the National Incomes Commission.

In 1965 George Brown produced the Joint Statement of Intent, with a 3 per cent to $3\frac{1}{2}$ per cent pay norm, and set up the National Board for Prices and Incomes. In 1966 came a six-month wage freeze followed by six months of 'severe restraint', which was gradually relaxed. It loosened further in 1968 and 1969 and was abandoned in 1970.

Two years later came Edward Heath's three-month pay freeze, six months of £1 a week plus 4 per cent, and finally 7 per cent plus indexation. This was scuppered in 1974 by the miners and the general election, which brought in the Labour Party and its 'social contract'. On its failure that was superseded in 1975 by a £6 a week limit, then £2.50 to £4, and finally a 1977 limit of 10 per cent (which produced a 15 per cent wage rise). Then came 'flexibility' and productivity bonuses, which were all abandoned on the change of government in 1979.

The long record shows that income policies do not survive for more than four years, and seldom that long. It also shows that they have a brief effect on pay scales but tend to be followed by dambursts to re-establish trends and differentials, or to conform to circumstances and expectations. Despite the repeated failure to control pay or to suppress inflation by restricting pay rises, demands to have another go crop up regularly.

Indexation

Linking something like investments, prices, wages, contributions etc to the rate of inflation.

Indices

See FT Index.

Individual Savings Accounts (ISAs)

Introduced as replacement of Tessas and Peps as the latest version of the government's attempt to persuade people to save by tax incentives, but not in a way that would make them reclaim too much.

From April 1999 the rules permit holding up to £50,000 in an ISA built up at no more than £5,000 a year. The money can go into unit trusts, shares or National Savings, with the dividend from shares holdable tax-free for the first five years.

Inflation

As most people are only too keenly aware inflation means that prices rise and money loses its value. The causes and effects are the subjects of heated argument as much among economists as laymen.

Traditional economics said that there were two main causes. One is manufacturing costs rising and so working through to user prices (called cost push inflation). The trigger could be fuel costs like oil, raw materials such as copper, or labour. The other cause was reckoned to be demand outstripping supply, which caused buyers to bid up the price of goods (called demand pull inflation). Monetarists (qv) added the third cause of too fast growth in the amount of money in circulation.

A persistent worry in Britain has been wages rising faster than productivity, which has generated a self-feeding spiral of expectations.

Some inflation is accepted by most countries as harmless, perhaps even helpful in keeping the economy buoyant, but that is generally below 3 per cent.

Inflation accounting

People automatically allow for inflation: 'it cost me £12 but that was six years ago, so heaven knows what it would cost now.' Yet company accounts pretend it never happened. That has not blunted its impact, merely misled managers and investors. Decades of acrimonious argument about the best way to adjust accounts caused accountants to stagger from one proposal to another without getting anything more than argument. Getting no help from journalists and analysts (they ignored inflation-adjusted figures), the Stock Exchange or the Inland Revenue (which did nothing to enforce their use), the accountants gave in. Though still proclaiming the importance of adjusting accounts, they made inclusion in the published figures voluntary. Sensible companies adjust management accounts but if they do not heed the result they distribute capital in dividend, with the inevitable result that they have to raise more cash with rights issues. During the 1980s and 1990s, lower inflation muted the argument and when the effect was reduced people thought it had disappeared.

Insider

The whole point of share dealing (like betting on horses) is that one person feels that he has a better idea of how a company will perform than the other party to the transaction. But under the new City morality this is permissible only if the feeling is wrong or based on guesswork. From 1980 it became illegal for anybody to deal if they had access to confidential price-sensitive information not available to the other side of the bargain. The insiders with this information are generally employees, directors, accountants, civil servants, and financial advisers. What is confidential and how one can prove knowledge were harder questions, it seems, for in the subsequent years hundreds of investigations of prima facie strong cases of dealing on leaked information produced an average of one successful prosecution per annum, and most of them succeeded only because the dealers confessed.

International Bank for Reconstruction and Development

The official name for the World Bank (qv).

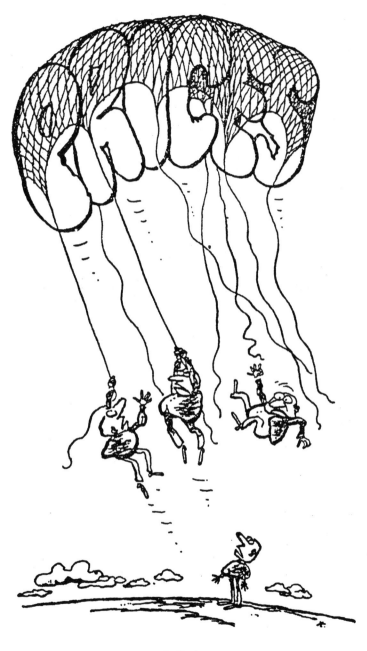

Inflation

International Monetary Fund

One of the two survivors of the Bretton Woods agreement (qv), the other being the World Bank (qv). The fund is in fact a bank to smooth fluctuations of the world trade cycle, to prevent a united plunge into the depression which afflicted major nations in the 1930s.

Each member country contributes a quota of special drawing rights and its currency, which the fund lends to countries troubled by short-term balance of payments or currency instability.

In the money

If the price of a share is above the level at which a call option – the right to buy a share – can be exercised then it (and its owner) are in the money.

Investment banks

US merchant banks. Some of the British banks, trying to get a share of the glamour which comes from efficiency and profit the US companies have, call themselves investment banks.

Investment clubs

Small investors are not liked on the stock exchange, despite all the publicity to the contrary. They take up the broker's time yet give only small orders, which are inadequate compensation. They make work for registrars of shareholders. They increase the burden on companies in sending out reports and dividends. They ask awkward questions at annual meetings, and they make a fuss if the money is lost. Anyone who doubts that need only look at the cost and convenience of dealing in shares.

It is also probably unwise for a small investor to sink money into individual companies because without the spread of shares among industries, economies and sizes, the nest-egg is too vulnerable. Pooling investments has been the way round that – hence the popularity of investment and unit trusts. Another way is for the individuals to club together, agree a broad strategy and pay a regular amount into a fund to buy shares.

There are over 1,000 of them in the UK and under the rules they can have between three and 20 members – above that and the club must be formed into a limited company.

Investment Management Regulatory Organization (IMRO)

The Financial Services Act 1985 aimed to protect investors from the more unscrupulous City sharks by getting the specialists to keep a beady eye on their own sectors of the business and discipline the shady operators. IMRO was one of those bodies which are responsible to the overall body, the Securities and Investments Board. Both of them have been replaced by the Financial Services Authority.

Investment trusts

Some companies make things, some provide services. An investment trust is a company like any other except that its sole purpose is to invest in other companies. Its shares are traded on the stock market in the normal way, with the price reflecting the success of the managers. The charm of such shares for the small investor is the spread across companies and even industries that a single investment provides. A curiosity is that the share price is often below the asset value of the investments owned, so they tend to get taken over for the break-up value.

They differ from unit trusts (qv) in being quoted, having a fixed number of shares and a price that is not directly related to the current value of the shares held.

Investors in Industry

Holding company of Industrial and Commercial Finance Corporation, Finance Corporation for Industry and Technical Development Capital, which make up the largest venture capital organization in Britain. It has taken to calling itself 3i.

Invisible hand

The locus classicus of free market economics: the belief that, left alone, the demand and supply decisions of individuals produces the balance people actually do want. It was spelled out by Adam Smith (1723–90) in his explanation that people pursuing self-interest would be led as if by an invisible hand to benefit society as a whole. A manufacturer desiring profit must supply goods the community wants at attractive prices, while workers and capital are pulled into most-needed areas by the greatest rewards.

> Every individual endeavours to employ his capital so that its produce may of the greatest value. He generally neither intends to promote the public interest, nor knows how much he is promoting it. He intends only his own security, only his own gain. And he is in this led by an invisible hand to promote an end which was no part of his intention. By pursuing his own interest he frequently promotes that of society more effectively than when he really intends to promote it.

(See also Laissez faire.)

Invisibles

Not the world of leprechauns or delirium tremens, merely international trade in services as opposed to visible goods. The term covers banking, insurance, and shipping (which are Britain's biggest invisible exports); tourism; dividend from overseas investment; results of foreign exchange and commodities trading; air transport; money from patents, profits from films, records, books and the like; royalties and copyrights. Britain is one of the few countries with a positive balance on sales of patents and know-how, though it is falling, and the general surplus on invisibles has offset the persistent deficit on trade.

Issuing house

What these institutions issue is shares on behalf of companies trying to raise capital. This can be either through the company issuing shares direct to the public, in which case the issuing house underwrites it (qv), or by the house buying the shares itself and then making an offer for sale. The 51 merchant bank members of the Issuing Houses Association (founded in 1945) are responsible for half the issues on the London Stock Exchange, the rest being mainly organized by stockbrokers. Clearly, the work represents only a small portion of a merchant bank's work.

J curve

When a country's currency depreciates against others, its exports become cheaper and so should boom, while imports become dearer, which should cause them to decline. This will boost the balance of payments but the initial effect is negative.

This is partly because, through inertia, it takes time for people to abandon even more expensive imports, and partly because imported raw materials to cope with demand are also more expensive.

So until the goods start leaving the country the balance of payments can dip and this short downturn, followed by a long rise, looks like a backward-leaning J – hence the name of the curve.

Jobbers

The people who make the stock market work, hazarding their own cash and setting the prices, were called stockjobbers, or jobbers for short. The term has been replaced by market-maker (qv) to show that the function has changed, and the jobber is often one arm of a financial group.

Journalese

City pages of newspapers are written in code and it helps to know the true meanings:
'Mr X alleged/Mr X claimed' = only libel laws prevent me pointing out that X is a notorious liar who is trying it on again.

'Mr X explained' = X is a goody and his is the side of the story I support.

'Controversial proposal' = I don't like the idea.

'Widespread concern' = as above.

'Widely welcomed reform' = I like the idea.

'Surprise announcement' = I failed to anticipate this one; = I said the opposite would happen.

'Caught the City off-guard' = my forecast was way out.

'As expected' = I recently wrote about this and got it right.

'City opinion' = the stockbroker/banker/journalist-at-the-next desk I spoke to this afternoon, said.

'It is believed that' = the person who leaked said for goodness' sake don't quote me.

'Technical reasons' = such complicated economics that neither I nor the person telling me understood, so you poor readers stand no chance; = we cannot think of any good reason.

'Irresponsible' (used by spokesmen) = right but embarrassing.

'Tendentious' = as above.

'Speculative' (from spokesmen) = true, but leaked before we were ready to announce it; (of investment) = dead dodgy, they would sue us if we told you just how crooked and/or incompetent the managers are.

'Speculative stock' = a shady or disintegrating outfit run by crooks or incompetents: buy shares only if you can already see a mug to take them off you at a higher price.
'No comment' (from spokesmen) = probably true.

'I can neither confirm nor deny' = as above.

'People/sources close to' = director/minister refusing to have a leak traced back.

Junk bonds

A term originating in the United States to describe high-yielding 'securities' issued by corporations, which generate little confidence and represent a highly speculative purchase – in plain English, a gamble.

Keynes

John Maynard Keynes (1883–1946) was that rare bird – an economist who proved he knew how the system worked by amassing a considerable fortune, not only for himself but also for King's College, Cambridge. It has since been alleged that this was helped by insider information.

In addition to lecturing at Cambridge he advised governments (he was attached to the Treasury during both World Wars) and after World War I wrote a book, The Economic Consequences of the Peace, which condemned the short-sighted and ultimately doomed policies pursued by the Versailles Treaty.

But the book which overturned economic thinking and changed government attitudes to economic management was The General Theory of Interest and Money, published in 1936. It said laissez faire would not spontaneously produce full employment and governments should instead intervene to smooth fluctuations produced by capitalism.

He said that during depression people spend less because they are uncertain about where the next wage packet is coming from, and this cut in consumption aggravates the downturn. As more people are thrown out of work the cycle is self-perpetuating and can be broken only by state intervention through spending to get movement into the economy.

For 40 years after the book's publication the world experienced no slumps and, when the hiccup came, it was caused by an external factor – the Arab restrictions on oil. Whether stability was due principally to Keynes is still argued, but at the very least he broadened economic thinking and the arguments are still principally between his followers and the natural reaction to his views.

The quality of his intellect may be judged by the reaction of Bertrand Russell: 'When I argued with him I felt I took my life in my hands and seldom emerged without feeling something of a fool.'

Kondratieff cycle

See Cycles.

Krugerrand

There is a widespread atavistic desire to own gold in preference to other measures of wealth. French and Arabs have been notorious gold hoarders for ages. Many countries forbid ownership of bullion, which drove people to coins such as Napoleons and sovereigns. But these are more expensive than the gold content would warrant so to fill the gap the non-communist world's largest producer of gold, South Africa, started in 1966 to mint its coins for this market. Each contains one ounce of gold but its weight is slightly more because of alloys used to produce an acceptable hardness. In Britain VAT makes the ownership on-shore less attractive. Opposition to apartheid has provoked a number of competitors from other countries ranging from Canada to the Isle of Man.

L

Laffer curve

Arthur Laffer, a young supply-side (qv) economist at the University of Southern California, achieved instant fame when, during a lunch with a journalist in 1974, he drew a curve on a napkin to illustrate the reasonable proposition that increasing tax rates does not necessarily increase total tax revenue. Tax paid will rise to a peak but beyond a certain level becomes burdensome. Then people feel it more efficient to spend time avoiding tax rather than making money: pay scales are distorted, jobs are exported, perks spread, non-financial benefits increase, and good brains work on tax avoidance schemes.

In most industrialized countries lowering income tax should therefore generate a higher yield. After long arguments among politicians and academics, the United States and Britain tried it and found the theory true.

Laissez faire

This French phrase, meaning let alone or leave free to act (sometimes written laisser faire), has become the label for a class of economics and politics opposed to state intervention in industrial and private economic activity: the extreme of unfettered capitalism. The origin is thought to have been in reply to the 17th-century French statesman Colbert asking merchants what they wanted from government. Legend has the reply as 'Laissez faire, laissez passer', meaning roughly, leave it alone, let things happen. Another attribution is to d'Argenson, a minister of Louis XV. The 19th-century advocates of laissez faire were probably reacting to the corrupt and inefficient governments of the previous two centuries. The most famous proponent,

Adam Smith, reckoned that individuals are the best judges of what they need and left to it would enrich not just themselves but the whole community (see Hidden hand). Interference with this natural order would merely diminish total wealth. Laissez faire was not claimed to replace all government. Smith said: 'defence is more important than opulence'; Carlyle said: 'anarchy plus the constable'; and Jeremy Bentham, while urging that government should 'stand out of the sunshine' of industry, added that it should fix 'the mechanisms of exchange in order that the forces of society may act freely'.

Lame ducks

Originally another Stock Exchange beast: a jobber who could not meet his obligations. Now a general expression for the hopeless and helpless. One recurrent political argument in Britain is about the extent to which the state should supply crutches to legless industrial ducks.

Laundering

In financial circles, the need for cleansing indicates a lot of dirt. Laundering in this context describes the process of shifting illegally gained cash through accounts or transactions to disguise its source. The money might come from drugs, miscellaneous crime, or massive black economy income.

Leading indicator

Some statistical series are reckoned to give an indication of where the economy is heading. Factory orders are one and share prices another (on the assumption that investors trade on the basis of how the companies will perform in about a year's time). To trust the indicators, especially when packaged into groups as governments tend to use them, it is best to see whether the supposed prescience of, say, share buyers still holds good, and whether any special factors have intervened since last time.

Leverage

US for gearing (qv).

LIBOR

See London inter-bank offered rate.

Liquidator

This word has acquired the thrilling aura of ruthless murder by silent KGB thugs. In commerce it is still elimination, but the only fatality is a company not its owners. When a corporation is so obviously moribund nothing can save it, shareholders, creditors, or a court can appoint someone to organize the obsequies. This liquidator has the task of selling corporate assets – stocks, materials, trade marks, patents, factories, machinery, etc – and distributing the proceeds among creditors. There is a strict hierarchy for payment, with holders of ordinary shares near the bottom and usually getting little or nothing. A receiver (qv) is appointed to keep the company running while its is reorganized or sold, but the latter keeps the business a going concern only if it helps get a higher price for the sale since their job is to turn it all into cash.

Listing

Getting a quote on the Stock Exchange. About 2 100 British companies, and 500 from overseas are currently listed in London, plus 300 on the Alternative Investment Market (qv).

Lloyd's

Lloyd's is one of several City institutions born in a coffee house. City merchants used to meet sea captains in Edward Lloyd's 17th-century coffee house in Tower Street and started insuring their cargoes. The aggressively 20th-century current home is still filled with booths replicating the wooden high-backed benches of its origins, and the commissionaires are still called waiters. The apostrophe in the name is also a relic of the original coffee house title.

There were over 33 000 Lloyd's individual members at the peak, who put up all their private capital to back insurance policies – since they pledge unlimited personal liability they could in theory be called on for their last penny to make losses good. This total declined rapidly as huge losses forced thousands into penury and persuaded many sleek cats to head for the shore.

An avalanche of frauds, rows and scandals covering hundreds of millions of pounds emerged in the late 1970s and provoked a special Act of Parliament to tighten regulation, but nobody went to jail. While profits continued, members flocked in. When in the 1980s that turned into thousands of millions of pounds of losses, the departures started by the reduced tax benefits turned into mass exodus.

In 1994 Lloyd's abandoned three centuries of tradition to allow in corporate members to make good the gap, and then found that a lot cheaper to administer. By 1998 individual membership had fallen to 6 800.

Members group themselves into 155 syndicates to get greater joint underwriting capacity. Insurance brokers wanting cover for a supertanker, satellite, fleet of airliners, or factory, wander about syndicate booths dealing with their class of business until they get the best price, though it may involve protracted bargaining. The first underwriter to accept the deal has to be a respected expert in that class of underwriting to persuade others to accept the same terms. Each syndicate underwriter will sign for a small percentage of the total risk, and the brokers tour the boxes until they build up 100 per cent. This is moving onto computers like the rest of City trade.

Originally best known for marine insurance, Lloyd's underwriters will take on almost anything, and it was the buccaneering independence from administration or supervision that helped to pioneer new business. They also accept reinsurance from all over the world to permit insurance companies to lay off some risks in major policies.

Loan Guarantee Scheme

Another government incentive (see Enterprise Investment Scheme) to assist new businesses to get going. When banks are reluctant to lend for a young company they can refer to the Department of Trade and Industry (DTI) for a guarantee of part of the loan if it meets a set of simple criteria. The DTI takes a percentage fee for this insurance, which makes the money relatively expensive.

Loan stock

Often this is used as an alternative name for debentures, and the two are similar in ranking high for repayment, being both classed as creditors, and being eligible for interest whether the company is making a profit or not. But debentures are usually secured against an asset, while loan stocks are unsecured (see also Debentures, Equities).

Lombard rate

Those sharp renaissance Italians have left an indelible mark on the world of banking. Not only the word 'bank', but the Lombardy origin is still evident in London's Lombard Street, which got its name from the Italians who set up shop there in the 15th century. The West German rate of interest at which the central Bundesbank lends to commercial banks when the loans are against top-rated securities such as Treasury Bills or bills of exchange is called the Lombard rate.

London inter-bank offered rate (LIBOR)

The interest rate top-rate banks in London will pay each other for Eurodollars. Lending in the Euromarket is frequently hitched to the three- or six-month LIBOR floating rate.

London International Financial Futures and Options Exchange (LIFFE)

When the predictable world of Bretton Woods (qv) was replaced by market fluctuations, industrialists needed ways of limiting damage from changes in currency and interest rates. Chicago opened a currency futures market in 1972 and extended the range of traded instruments over the years but it was not until 1982 London followed suit with LIFFE (pronounced 'life', presumably to avoid giving the impression that the exchange is in Dublin).

It was Karl Marx who pointed out that money was the 'commodity of commodities' and indeed LIFFE is much like any futures market (qv): one buys and sells currencies, gilts, three-month deposits, or takes a bet on the Stock Exchange 100 Share Index, all for some specified time in the future but priced at a value agreed today.

As with other such markets, the primary aim is not to take delivery but to cover a dangerous trade exposure or to have a gamble. For instance, a company with a predicted need for borrowing at an identified time can safeguard against rising interest rates by selling financial futures contracts (selling short (qv)) for the borrowing date so that if interest rates do rise it will be able to make a profit on the appreciation of the financial futures as a way of offsetting the higher cost of borrowing.

Unlike the stock market, LIFFE operates by 'open outcry' –
ie an unseemly screaming scrimmage.

London Metal Exchange (LME)

Very much what the name implies – a place where metals are
traded in London, with much of the business done in futures
(qv). The metals dealt in are copper, zinc, tin, lead, silver and
aluminium. The LME is by City standards a relative newcomer,
having been founded in 1881. The core of the exchange is the
'ring', about 12 feet across, round which sit representatives of
the main metal dealers. Over three-quarters of the seats are
controlled by traders in which overseas companies have an
interest. Members must produce £500 000 security plus the same
again as bank guarantee.

Trading starts at noon and finishes at 1.10 pm and continues
from 3.30 to 4.35 pm, though unofficial deals go on for an extra
20 minutes after each session and thereafter on the telephone.
This is 'late kerb trading', so called from the days when they
really were conducted at the kerb outside the exchange.

The LME also sets the standard quality of metals traded. Only
5 per cent of world metals trade passes through the LME, with
New York overshadowing it for copper and influence on silver
price, and Penang trading more tin. However, the LME still has
influence on world metal prices.

Long run

One of Keynes's best known aphorisms was his retort to
economists who kept going on about the long term: 'in the long
run we are all dead.' Now frequently used by politicians who
have seldom planned beyond tea time and never further than
the next election.

London Metal Exchange

M0, M1, M2, M3 etc

See Money supply.

Macmillan gap

In 1929 the government set up one of a long series of committees to look at finance in the UK. It purported to be a monetary commission to look at the way the Bank of England conducted monetary policy, and its report did indeed lead to a much more tightly managed economy.

A part of the report however, pointed to the problems of smaller companies in raising risk capital, and the high cost of what they could get. A regular series of commissions and less official investigations followed over the subsequent seven decades repeating the finding in amusingly similar terms. Attempts by governments to do something about this have included a range of tax incentive schemes and instigating the creation of a venture capital institution now called 3i. The gap remains.

Manpower Services Commission (MSC)

Yet another of the proliferating government agencies. Set up under the Employment and Training Act 1973, the MSC is supposed to train people for jobs. It has in turn spawned the Employment Service Agency and the Training Services Agency.

Mareva injunction

Legal measure to stop debtors spiriting their assets out of reach of creditors and the law. Named after a judgment in *Mareva Compania Naviera SA v International Bulkcarriers SA* (1975) which was overlooked by all the experts at the time – the All England Law Reports woke up to its significance only five years later. In fact, a decision earlier the same year in *Nippon Yusen Kaisha v Karageorgis* had already come to the same conclusion.

Margin call

Gamblers in the futures markets are obliged to put up a relatively small collateral (unless they can lodge other form of security) and this is called the margin. If the price moves against the dealer, the broker will ask for additional funds to maintain the ratios and this is called a margin call.

Mark

In the Stock Exchange the mark is not always the much-desired German currency, usually it is the price at which a deal was carried out. When prices are being marked down, market-makers are lowering prices when faced with apathy or selling, and vice versa.

Market capitalization

See Capitalization.

Market-maker

The people who set the prices for shares by dealing on their own behalf, formerly called jobbers, are now called market-makers. (The change of name was just public recognition of the fact that jobbers are no longer the independent traders but arms of financial conglomerates which also own brokers.) They will take stock onto their books when people are selling and perhaps 'go short' (sell more stock than they have) when there is a spate of buying.

They display buying and selling prices on the Stock Exchange's SEAQ computer (qv) and the size of deal they will accept. Every broker can call up on screen the price set by each jobber and is obliged to deal 'at best execution'. Some of the major financial institutions also get the SEAQ service and can deal direct.

Say the market-maker displays 60p for buying and 64p for selling and they get a surge of brokers buying from them. If they have sold short, they may have to raise their prices to say 61p to 65p to attract sellers. If that succeeds and they pick up the shares at 61p, they have made 3p per share on the deal and that is called their 'turn' – ie profit.

Market-makers live on their ability to anticipate the market mood and shift prices accordingly, as well as to widen or narrow the 'spread' (difference between buying and selling price) to counteract a one-way market. The cost of holding stocks on their books at times of high interest rates began to erode profit on jobbing and contributed to the Stock Exchange's abandonment of its age-old separation of the broking and market-making functions.

Mean

In the statistical sense, see Average.

Merchant banks

'Banks who are not merchants, merchants who are not banks, and houses who are neither merchants nor banks' is one disenchanted view of these organizations. The name arose from their trading origins though they diversified into finance, generally acceptances, and are now exclusively financial institutions. They tend to deal with companies (or very rich individuals); they have high prestige but are relatively small (though growing with the addition of other financial services such as stockbroking); and they organize others to lend to companies. So merchant banks are issuing houses (qv), accepting houses (qv), organize eurocurrency loans (qv), advise on acquisitions and corporate finance, and they run unit trusts and portfolio management.

Mezzanine finance

As its name implies it is a sort of intermediate, bastard concept, in this case between debt and equity funding for a company. It can be considered either as expensive debt or as cheap equity, depending on whether the issuing company looks on mezzanine as convertible loan stocks, an issue of subordinated debt, or a type of preference share. In practice it is that portion of finance which is too risky or has too little solid collateral to produce loans from the banks but is paying too little to attract equity. It is therefore a bit like debt but lower down the hierarchy of safety from senior debt (qv) provided by banks, while being better secured and earning less than ordinary shares.

Middle market price

There are two prices for each share on the Stock Exchange: one at which one can buy and the other which one can sell, with the market-maker getting their living from the difference (see Spread). Apart from special valuations, such as tax or probate, the average of the two is used to indicate the price and is the one newspapers list.

Minimum Lending Rate (MLR)

The authorities are for ever vacillating between pretending that interest rates are set exclusively by the market, and admitting that they are controlled by the government and the Bank of England. In practice, however, it is a mixture and MLR is announced on Thursdays.

MIRAS

Mortgage interest relief at source – repayments being net of tax relief.

Mode

See Average.

Monetarist

'History offers ample evidence that what determines the average level of prices and wages is the amount of money in the economy and not the greediness of business or workers.' That is probably the most concise encapsulation of the monetarist view and comes from the arch-priest of the cult, Professor Milton Friedman (in *Capitalism and Freedom*). In *Free to Choose*, Professor Friedman set out his thesis:

1. Inflation is a monetary phenomenon arising from a more rapid increase in the quantity of money than in output.
2. In today's world government determines – or can determine – the quantity of money.
3. There is only one cure for inflation: a slower rate of increase in the quantity of money.
4. It takes time – measured in years not in months – for inflation to develop; it takes time for inflation to be cured.
5. Unpleasant side effects of the cure are unavoidable.

But, if challenged, he concedes, 'undoubtedly there can be and are influences running both ways' – incomes influence the quantity of money as well as vice versa.

Opponents agree with point 5 but deny such simple causal links, and say the direction of effect is harder to establish than Professor Friedman says. Governments also find they must respond to demands for money, or alternatives take its place. Lord Kaldor showed that in Britain 74 per cent of the deviation from long-term money supply trends is caused by public sector deficits.

In sum, monetarists say when governments spend more than they raise in taxes the difference comes from 'printing' money (in fact they borrow from individuals and the banking system and print Treasury Bills and gilts). This extra cash in the system bids up prices, which is inflation. Keynesians contend that extra cash could stimulate commerce and production instead and the New Cambridge School says that sudden rises in demand just attract imports. And both point out that if individuals buy government stock, money supply does not increase.

All may have a germ of truth – simple explanations of complex systems are always wrong. Whatever the truth of the monetarist theory, it is salutary for policy-makers to remember Goodheart's First Law: 'the claim that relationships between monetary aggregates and other aggregates persists precisely to the extent that such relationships are not exploited.'

Monetary compensation amounts (MCA)

One of the fiddles trying to offset the inadequacies and distortions of the EEC Common Agricultural Policy (qv) – it is a tax or subsidy to offset the differentials between 'green' and real exchange rates. The green rate (as in Green pound (qv)) is used to calculate farm prices and hence subsidies but is relatively fixed, being revalued only when politically expedient or when international pressure demands it. Actual currencies move in response to the market. To bridge the gap between real currency values and farming calculations a temporary adjustment is used. When a currency appreciates against those of other EEC countries it gets a positive MCA, and vice versa, to maintain price equality. In other words, MCA subsidizes food imports for weak currency countries by bringing down prices. Member governments have agreed to phase out the system.

Money-purchase pensions

Sometimes also called defined contribution schemes because the amount paid in is known and fixed but the eventual pension received is anyone's guess. The actual amount paid out depends on the amount invested and how well, what charges the administrator levies, and what the annuity rates are at the time of retirement. The other sort is the final salary type (qv).

Money supply

Mentions of M1, M2 or M3 in the City pages of newspapers are not discussions of motorway madness but measures of various definitions of how much money there actually is in the economy. Professor Milton Friedman of Chicago, most prominent of the latest generation of monetarist economists (though the quantity theory of money has a venerable history), leads a school of thought that says inflation is a direct if delayed result of increasing too quickly the amount of money in the economy.

The problem is that defining money is difficult, especially in a sophisticated economy which uses a wide range of financial instruments.

M0 includes coins and notes in circulation; M1 covers that plus the private sector sterling current accounts; M2 is hazy and not much used in the UK, though Americans do use it; M3 is M1 plus other term deposits such as deposit accounts in banks, deposits at discount houses, and other interest-bearing accounts including public sector deposits but excluding UK residents' foreign currency deposits. Definitions have been evolved for M4, M5, and even M6 but such things are restricted to addicts.

As one would expect, M1 and M3 normally move in parallel but from time to time there is a divergence, some of which is explicable by movements in interest rates, but some leave experts frankly baffled.

Sir Claus Moser, when head of the Central Statistical Office, warned that 'any figure that looks interesting is probably wrong'. There is also Goodheart's Second Law, which says that 'any measure of the money supply that is officially controlled promptly loses its meaning'.

Monopoly

Two ways of making lots of money are to sell a board game that stays popular for generations, or to control a market so completely that one can charge what one like. Both go under the name of Monopoly.

The board game is actually about property development and has nothing to do with its name. Strictly speaking, a monopoly supplier has no competitors. British legislation has never taken the word literally, and the Fair Trading Act 1973 defined it as having as little as a quarter of the market (see Oligopoly).

Monopoly power is usually diluted by the availability of alternatives. With the growing internationalization of trade only protected state monopolies can exploit their market power without attracting overseas competition.

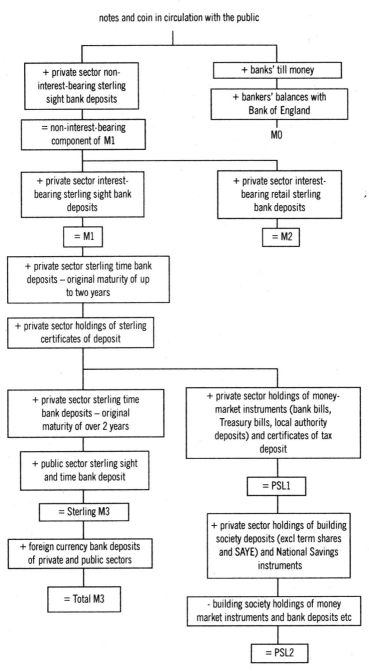

Money supply

Monopoly

Monopsony

Monopoly is a market in which there is one supplier (eg railways), but there are some markets in which there is only one buyer, and economists have dubbed this monopsony. Predictably, such market distortions are usually reserved for government and state enterprises. In theory, international trade should mitigate such power since suppliers should be able to sell in other countries but in practice manufacturers are usually so fettered by the specifications dictated by the giant public sector buyers that the goods are not acceptable overseas, which makes the state buyer absolute. Military equipment is in a similar position. In addition, governments often exert their buying power to structure the supplying industry – airframes, aero-engines, telephone exchanges – and set not just product standards but profit levels as well.

Mortgage

This is nothing more complicated than a fancy specialist name for a loan to buy a home. The standard format sets a limit, such as 20 or 25 years, during which the loan is serviced with interest payments plus a repayment of the capital. As it is set for a steady level of payment – though fluctuating with interest levels – in the initial years most of the repayment money is interest and in the final years the payments are almost all capital.

As governments have always believed a property-owning populace is likely to be boringly bourgeois, with a stake in stability, mortgages have been given tax relief. As the figure reached 80 per cent, that loss of tax revenue came increasingly to be questioned by chancellors wanting more tax. So the amount of tax allowance has been gradually whittled by chancellors and inflation.

Mutual organization

An organization such as a building society or friendly society jointly owned by its members who therefore get all the benefits and profits from the activities. Many of the larger building society managers found this too restrictive for their ambitions and bribed owners with bonuses and free shares to allow conversion into incorporated companies. For these, the profits go outside the business in the form of dividends to shareholders who may be financial institutions with no interest in the customers or borrowers. 'Carpet-baggers' opened accounts in all the major societies in the hope of a windfall when the managers' megalomania transformed yet another mutual.

Naked option

Only financial flash: it means taking a position on the options market without a protective position in the opposite direction.

National Economic Development Office (NEDO)

Selwyn Lloyd, when Chancellor of the Exchequer in 1961, had the revolutionary notion that governments should plan ahead and that they might do that better if industrialists and unions told them what was happening. The NED Council was the forum created, and in 1964 the Labour Government used it as the medium for a National Plan. That was such an ignominious failure that it discredited planning.

But NEDO survived and committees were set up to look after industrial sectors, publishing guides and trying to nudge them into greater effectiveness. With little record of concrete achievement the whole establishment was gradually whittled in size and influence until Mrs Thatcher finally delivered the *coup de grâce*.

National Institute for Economic and Social Research (NIESR)

Peering into the economic future is a popular sport, with dozens of organizations attempting it regularly, but the NIESR is taken more seriously than most. Set up in 1938 as a non-profit research body, it has had close relations with the Treasury in constructing computer models of the economy. Despite that, the two often disagree on both policy and prospects. Economic forecasts cannot be right because the statistics are out of date (like driving a car by looking through the rear-view mirror), and governments change circumstances. NIESR forecasts are on the basis of unaltered public policy but since the Chancellor may act as a result of the forecast it is hard to tell whether the organization was right.

National insurance

Another form of income tax, but with another name to hide the true impact. It is a progressive tax (the percentage paid rises with income) but only up to a ceiling amount.

National loan fund rate

Yet another standard for interest rates (see also Treasury bill rate, Minimum Lending Rate, Base rate). It is the rate at which central government is prepared to lend to nationalized industries and local authorities, and is related to gilt yield and hence derives from the government's own manipulation of the money market.

Negative equity

The difference between the size of a mortgage and the market value of a home – the bit one actually owns – is often described as the homeowner's equity. When property prices tumble and the value drops below the mortgage amount, the householder has negative equity.

Negative income tax

Very poor people can be helped by incorporating PAYE income tax with social security benefits so those earning above the threshold pay income tax normally but those below receive money to bring them up to a minimum guaranteed income. This is called negative income tax and its advocates say that benefits taper off with rising incomes rather than disappear suddenly at set levels (as happens now), so the system does not deter people from earning more through fear of being pushed into that gap between earnings and benefits. It is therefore said to avoid the poverty trap (qv).

Net present value

See Cash flow.

Newly industrialized economies

Usually used to describe four Far Eastern countries which are really getting the hang of becoming rich: Hong Kong, Taiwan, South Korea and Singapore.

Nikkei

The Tokyo stock market index of the blue chip shares roughly equivalent to London's FT Ordinary Index.

Nominee holding

Bashful investors can buy shares through a merchant bank or stockbroker and register the holding through specially constituted companies which will appear on the share register. A company can ask for the beneficial ownership of nominee holdings but in the case of small holdings seldom does. Even when it does the answers are rarely published so some degree of anonymity remains. Holdings of over 5 per cent must be declared.

Non-voting shares

A few companies have two sets of shares – usually called A and B – with voting restricted to one, usually the smaller set. The aim is to retain control of the company in the hands of its original owners. The price of the non-voting shares is lower to offset the normal rights of shareholders to control directors. Companies coming to the market are discouraged from such arrangements and most of the companies have enfranchised both classes, paying voting holders appropriate compensation.

Ofex

Contraction of 'off exchange', meaning trading in shares other than through the conventional stock market computer. The J Jenkins stockbroking company operates its own computerized trading, with lower fees and fewer admittance requirements to allow speculative and young companies to find a market for their shares.

Off balance sheet finance

Some perfectly legitimate but a few rather suspect reasons are used by companies to finance investment in a way that does not show in the statutory accounts. Leasing is the most straightforward and common. But there are circuitous devices including apparently totally separate companies for raising money to fund specific ventures, which are used when a company is already up against its borrowing limits or just does not want its balance sheet to look too sick. The accountancy profession is plugging loopholes as it spots them.

Oligopoly

Genuine monopolies are rare. Far more usual is a market controlled by a small number of companies. These situations are usually called near-monopolies or almost monopolies, but the correct term is oligopoly. Examples of this are the banking system, in which five or six groups have almost all the branches; detergents, in which Procter & Gamble and Unilever are dominant; petrol, with some five companies having much of the business; sugar, newsprint, and cigarettes are other examples.

The Monopolies and Mergers Commission is entitled to examine a company with over 25 per cent of a market. But as the City graffito runs: 'How come there is only one Monopolies Commission?'

On the run

Not the broker – few of them have been found out so they have not yet been forced to flee from the police – this refers to the most recently issued Treasury Bills (qv), which have three, six or twelve months to run. Sometimes extended to top Japanese banks' issues of Certificates of Deposit.

Open outcry

An understatement for the method of trading on some markets such as the London International Financial Futures and Options Exchange (qv). To the untutored eye that seems a disorderly mob of flashily dressed young people in a state of riot screaming their heads off at each other, waving their arms about in a grotesque exaggeration of tic-tac people, and hurling paper around. It is said to work, with the main virtue being that everybody knows what everyone else is up to.

Options

Options means choice, and in the context of the stock market it means the purchase of the right to make choice on whether to buy (or sell) a share. For instance, one may need to sell some shares soon and have to be certain the price will not plummet in the meantime. So one buys a 'put' option (qv), which is a contract conferring the right to sell those shares at a stated price (the striking price), which is generally the market price on the day the deal is arranged. The fee can be considered an insurance premium so if the price does drop the extra will have been worth it, and, if not, all one has lost is the option money. This is the way of protecting oneself by minimizing losses at times of price fluctuations and the system was known back in the 16th century. But it can also be used as a gamble: if one is pretty sure a company's share price will fall one can buy the put option without having any shares to sell. Then when the time comes in three months and the shares have fallen, they can be bought cheaply in the market and the option to sell exercised at the higher price. Conversely, if one is pretty sure the price will rise, one can buy a 'call' option (qv). That gives the right to buy the shares over the next three months at the agreed price, and sell them immediately at a profit. In both cases if the forecast turns out wrong, the loss is limited to the relatively small option money. There are also double and straddle options (qv) and there is yet another safeguard in being able to sell the option before the expiry date on the traded options market (qv) of the Stock Exchange. Options also exist in other markets.

Ordinary shares

These are also known as equities, and in the United States are called common stock. The owner of a company (the shareholder) is protected so their maximum loss is the value of their shares, and is not liable for the full debts of a company. That is why they are called limited liability companies, as opposed to partnerships, where the partners have unlimited liability. There are preferred ordinary shares (see Preference) and deferred ordinaries, which come near the bottom in the priorities for payment, after preferred.

Organization for Economic Cooperation and Development (OECD)

A research and chat club for rich nations set up to 'promote policies designed to achieve the highest sustainable economic growth and employment and a rising standard of living in member countries, while maintaining financial stability, and thus contribute to the development of the world economy; to contribute to sound economic expansion in member as well as non-member countries in the process of economic development; to contribute to the expansion of world trade on a multilateral, non-discriminatory basis in accordance with international obligations'. Modest aims. In fact, much of the time it co-ordinates statistics from members from which it derives forecasts for individual countries and for OECD as a whole. It also produces booklets on recondite topics ranging from fisheries to tourism, from educational policies to regional infrastructure for development. The members are Australia, Austria, Belgium, Britain, Canada, Denmark, Finland, France, Germany, Greece, Iceland, Japan, Luxembourg, Netherlands, New Zealand, Norway, Portugal, Spain, Sweden, Switzerland, Turkey and the United States.

Out of the money

Who isn't? In the stock market this is a more specific statement meaning that the current price of a share is lower than the price at which a call option (the right to buy) has been set. In other words, one would be out of the money (and out of one's mind) to exercise the option.

Overnight money

Nothing to do with bed and breakfast, overnight money is the brief deposit at a bank of largish sums, usually by large industrial corporations. It makes up a considerable portion of the interbank eurocurrency market.

Oversold

An optimistic view of a falling stock market: it is defined as a technical position where a sudden rush of selling has depressed prices below what would be justified in the circumstances. A dangerous view for the inexperienced, since it works on the assumption that one knows better than the market, whereas a share is in fact worth only what someone will pay for it.

Over the counter

At its simplest this is trade in shares outside the recognized and established stock markets. The organized market in unquoted securities really started in the United States in about 1926 and has now reached very large proportions. In Britain it started in 1972 and has since been taken on by a number of smaller licensed dealers who matched buyers and sellers, but a few do a little jobbing on their own account. The Stock Exchange has tried to pre-empt the need by starting the Alternative Investment Market (qv) for smaller and younger companies. That was far too costly for private companies which had only one or two transactions a year and some have gone instead onto Ofex (qv).

Pac-man defence

When a take-over target retaliates with an offer for the bidder it starts an eat-or-be-eaten battle which whimsical Americans considered similar to one of the early computer games.

Paper gold

Everything valuable is still related to the traditional measure of wealth – coal and oil have been called black gold and when Special Drawing Rights (qv) were invented they were dubbed paper gold.

Pareto's Law

About 100 years ago an Italian economist Vilfredo Pareto put into words what everybody has always known, that it is only a small portion of any activity that causes most work. So, for instance, 80 per cent of a company's sales go to 20 per cent of the customers, and 20 per cent of customers cause 80 per cent of the problems. Similarly, 20 per cent of stocks account for 80 per cent of turnover, and so on. This 80/20 rule, also called 'the law of the trivial many and the crucial few', is a guide to where effort should be concentrated. Picking the crucial bit is often called ABC analysis.

Parities

Just another term for rates of currency exchange.

Par value

See Value at par.

Pay policy

See Incomes policy.

P/E ratio

One of the many ways for assessing the rating of a company is the ratio of share price to earnings. This tells two things: how highly the company is regarded by other investors, and how many years profit at the current levels one would have to pay for in buying the shares.

To calculate the ratio, take the net profit of the company (after tax and charges) and divide it by the number of shares on issue. That gives earnings per share. Then divide it into the share price.

For instance, let us assume the earnings per share came out at 4p, and the shares currently stand at 40p. The P/E ratio is then 10. If the number is high, say upwards of 25, investors clearly think this is a wonderful company which will increase profits fast enough to offset the ludicrously high price the shares now command. A low P/E, by contrast, suggests that the market expects the company to fall over soon.

One advantage of the system is that it is common to both the United States and the United Kingdom, so investments across the Atlantic can be compared directly.

Perks

Directors have come in for prolonged criticism for being fat cats with huge pay rises irrespective of what the company does, plus enjoying the benefit of extensive perks. A growing number of the perks are being taxed as benefit in kind so some of the attraction is waning, but there are still a few loopholes.

Shareholders of some companies also get perks. P&O gives cut prices on its cross-Channel ferries, Groupe Chez Gérard sends out money-off vouchers for its restaurants, several hotel groups reduce the prices at hotels and so on. Shareholders get better deals on cars, wines, washing machines, motor exhausts, clothes, dry cleaning and food. Associated British Foods hands out a carrier bag full of goodies at its annual general meeting, and many retired investors turn up for such occasions at many companies only for the free meal and drinks.

Permanent health insurance

See Health insurance.

Personal equity plan (PEP)

A modest tax benefit to encourage shareholders to buy more equity but pretending to be a temptation for those who do not currently hold any shares. It was replaced by Individual Savings Accounts (qv).

Personal Investment Authority (PIA)

One of the regulating organizations spawned by the Financial Services Act. This one looked after the private investor until the job was taken over by the Financial Services Authority.

Petrodollars

Surplus cash sloshing around the coffers of oil exporters was called petrodollars. The state of the oil market determines the amount but it did rise to over $50 000 million and much was recycled back into the developed world, mostly into property and equities.

Phillips curve

Looking at wages and employment figures between 1861 and 1957, Professor A W Phillips concluded that workers got larger pay rises when unemployment was low. In other words, as workers became scarce, companies bid higher to get some. Conversely, with more jobless around, employees had less bargaining power. If unemployment rises enough pay rises should stop – any more out of work and wages fall. The graph demonstrating this relation is called the Phillips curve.

It follows that if unduly large pay increases cause inflation and the government cannot persuade workers to moderate demands, the way to stop the inflationary spiral is to increase unemployment. This course has been advocated by several economists.

But a Treasury study concluded that pay inflation is insensitive to unemployment levels 'over quite a wide band'; the National Institute for Economic and Social Research reckoned 'there is no way of knowing the scale of unemployment required to produce any given change in the inflation rate'; and in the US wage inflation was forecast to fall to zero at between 5 per cent and 10 per cent unemployment, though Britain passed that level with 3 million out of work but pay rises comfortably outpacing inflation.

Placing

There are five ways of issuing shares to the public. In a private placing all the shares available from the company are issued through a stockbroker to its wealthy clients, commonly the institutions such as insurance companies and pension funds. The company need not be quoted for this exercise, but if it is some of the shares must be made available to the public. Other methods of getting money from the market are a public issue with prospectus and underwriters, a rights issue giving existing holders a chance to buy more shares, offer for sale, and offer for sale by tender.

Poison pill

Directors dislike their company being taken over because they often lose their jobs. Hence they are tempted to put their own incomes ahead of shareholders' interests by erecting complex barriers to being acquired. Sometimes these change structure, sometimes they shift cash, sometimes it involves the issuing of paper whenever a bid goes through. This not only deters bidders (even if shareholders would like to be bought out at a high price) but can produce problems for the company.

Policyholder protection scheme

Set up under the Policyholders' Protection Act 1975 to compensate people whose insurance company has failed. Protection is up to 90 per cent of the benefits.

Poverty trap

A poor family is entitled to a range of state help such as reduced Council Tax, free school meals and various Social Security benefits. But if the family income rises the benefits are lost even if the extra wages are not enough to offset completely the loss of support. Without a tapering of means-tested benefits, a slight increase in income can actually leave a family worse off. That is a disincentive to extra effort because the gap between the income, which allows full benefits, and the earnings, which would fully compensate for their loss is wide – a pay rise may have to be substantial to leap across the gap. This gap is called the poverty trap. A tapering benefit like negative income tax (qv) has been proposed to get round the problem.

Pre-emption rights

The rights of existing shareholders to take part in their company's new shares issues to maintain the existing percentage holding. It is normally exercised when the business is trying to place shares either as part of a cash-raising exercise or as a result of a take-over for paper which the seller does not want (see Vendor placing).

Preference shares

What they are preferred to are ordinary shares because holders rank ahead for any dividend, normally at fixed interest but sometimes with entitlement to a minimum level and then a participation in the company's distributable profits. Preference holders also have priority for repayment on the break-up of the company (on insolvency, for example).

Premium

One meaning is simply the price over what the true value is taken to be. So, for instance, if an investment trust has a market price above the value of the underlying investments, it is said to stand at a premium. When the balance is the other way it is said to be at a discount.

Another meaning is the amount a policyholder gives the insurance company.

Price/earnings ratio

See P/E ratio.

Prices policy

The recurrent attempt by governments to stop water flowing down hill. Like wage control, it has a 3 700 year history of failure. Hamurabi, King of Babylon; Periclean Athens; the Roman emperors Diocletian and Julian all have tried to hold down prices, but as Confucius pointed out, the only way governments can stabilize prices is by bringing supply and demand into balance. In Britain the tradition goes back to 1199, when an attempt was made to control the wholesale and retail price of wine. It failed, as did the 1202 law to regulate wheat prices. More recent policies were prompted by high wage demands pushing up inflation so the price policy was a quid pro quo to buy union co-operation in moderating pay rises. During sluggish economic activity, prices are held down by competition; restraining them in an upturn may deny businesses the chance to accumulate fat for the lean years. Prices policies are admissions that the government cannot ensure sound competition, or the market cannot keep prices economic. Since the former is open to correction and the latter open to question, it is not surprising the policies have been largely ineffective.

Direct controls, like rationing, are just ways of organizing scarcity while ensuring it continues – a free market price system works to overcome scarcities.

Prime rate

The rate at which US banks lend to first class (prime) customers. Has similar guide function to the base rate in Britain.

Privatization

Returning nationalized industries to public hands. Sometimes, as with the Trustee Savings Banks, selling off to its owners what never belonged to the state in the first place. The best known privatizations in the UK have been of the utilities like gas, electricity, water and telephone. The advantage of the deal is the industries escape from the dead hand of government and the permanent restriction on investment capital, the disadvantage is the potential for exploiting command of a necessity to make profits for shareholders. Despite the extensive protests at leaving necessities at the mercy of a commercial marketplace, most of the industries have improved efficiency and produced better value since becoming publicly held.

Pro bono

This is an abbreviation of pro bono publico, which is a Latin tag meaning for the public good. It is the label rich directors and professionals give to their unpaid work taken on to show what good citizens they are. Others do the work without giving it a label.

Productivity

Productivity

Output per head attributable to employee effort is the common use of the word, with the implication that harder or better work would increase it. So if productivity is on a plateau, employers blame workers, and if it rises unions take the credit for their members. In fact productivity measures the efficiency of all factors of production – it is the relation between output of a plant (or office) and the input in labour, capital, materials etc. Most improvements in efficiency result from the installation of better machinery. In Britain this produced a long-term trend of nearly 3 per cent a year rise in productivity, and was therefore by far and away the major factor in economic growth.

Unions like productivity bargaining because it provides a watertight reason for a pay rise so they get a share of the corporation's extra investment benefits and then sell their restrictive practices. But in most industries, British output or added value per head is well below that of competing nations.

Protectionism

This is a policy of keeping out foreign-produced goods as a matter of principle – by imposing tariffs, quotas or restrictions. Advocates say it protects home producers, allowing them to survive and be profitable. It may be permanent because domestic businesses are incurably inefficient but usually it is seen as a temporary measure to allow native companies to grow strong enough to withstand international competition.

The Japanese have long pursued this policy covertly, in the UK it has been proposed to prevent overseas enterprises from attacking on a narrow front without leaving time for domestic manufacturers to adapt. But, like the measures against dumping (qv), it is not clear why domestic companies always lose while foreign producers can afford to buy market share with low prices. Opponents to protection point out the 1929–31 world slump was aggravated by defensive import barriers. Since economists are usually solving the last problem, they warn about the dangers of retaliatory protection precipitating another such recession. In fact, such 'tit for tat' has seldom ensued even in the face of open provocation. Consumers suffer from protection as they cannot buy from the cheapest producer, and industries suffer since there is no spur to improvement and efficiency. Free traders also argue that there is no point in every country trying to produce everything – each should concentrate on what it is best at and sell it to the others.

Proxy

A person acting in place of and on behalf of another. For instance, someone appointed by a shareholder to attend the annual general meeting and vote on their behalf. A company calling a meeting must tell shareholders they may appoint a proxy (who does not have to be a shareholder) and usually sends a card inviting them to nominate one of the directors. A shareholder may instruct the proxy how to vote or leave it to their discretion. Sometimes proxies may not vote by show of hands but only in a poll, which is why for controversial measures somebody generally demands a poll.

Public sector borrowing requirement

At the beginning of the 20th century deficit financing – the state spending more than it received – was thought fundamentally immoral. The new morality is monetarism and that focuses on state expenditure with equal censure.

Economists care not just about the size of the overspending but how it is incurred and how a cash shortfall is made good. Unless the government takes out of the economy (eg through savings) about the same amount it puts in, it may drive up prices. If the deficit is filled by borrowing from banks, that merely expands their lending base, which increases money supply, and hence could also jack up inflation.

If, on the other hand, the deficit is financed from the savings of companies and individuals there is no rise in money supply, interest rates could be pushed up through competition for savings, and that could lead to 'crowding out' of borrowing by industry. An additional problem is that during a downturn in the economy there are more jobless so there is less income tax coming in and more benefits paid out by the state; profits are down so there is less from corporation tax. As a result of all these government deficit is bound to grow. But if the government then cuts spending the recession is aggravated. This is a dilemma for monetarists,whose 'recipe for reducing inflation could slow the economy and so increase the deficit.

Put option

In the option market one pays a small price for the right to deal at a specified time in the future at today's price. Buying a put option gives the right to sell a fixed amount of, say, shares.

Put through

The Stock Exchange wants deals to go through the market rather than bypass its control by allowing investors to trade among themselves. So if a broker gets separate orders which by coincidence instruct them to buy and sell the same stock in roughly equal quantities, they must still put the deal through the market at best execution price.

Broker dealers will clearly just take the shares onto their own book and report the deal but agency brokers (who have no market-making activity) must put the deal through an established market-maker or organize a so-called cross – ie look around for a matching buyer or seller to complete the deal. As the risk element of taking on stock is absent, the spread between buying and selling prices should be narrower.

Quality of earnings

One would have thought quantity more important but shrewd analysts also check the probable stability of a company's income. Whether prosperity is fugitive or secure depends on the structure and state of the competition, trends in costs, and the need for research and change.

Quango

When the government wants the credit for success while avoiding the blame for failure, or wants more public servants without the total pay bill for the civil service going up, it creates Quangos. These are quasi-autonomous non-governmental organizations, whose staff are paid out of the taxpayer's purse but are not answerable to Parliament, eg the Equal Opportunities Commission. They proliferated wildly during the 1980s and 1990s.

Quantity theory of money

The amount of money in the economy multiplied by the number of times it changes hands in a year is the same as the volume of goods produced multiplied by their price. This obvious statement that purchases and sales are equal was reduced by the famous economist Irving Fisher to the formula $MV_{=}PT$. This was the precursor to monetarism (qv) as most economists reckon the velocity of circulation (V) is constant and the quantity of output (T) is inflexible in the short term, so a rise in money supply (M) equals a rise in prices (P). Simple and obvious – but untrue. For a start, nobody knows the velocity of circulation (it is usually a residual) and money has proved not to be a readily determinable entity.

Queen's Award for Industry

'Unto every one that hath shall be given and he shall have in abundance' says St Matthew, and so it is in business. Companies that have made a lot of money from exports or new technology get, in addition, the Queen's Award. It provides no cash or assistance, just the patriotic glow of royal recognition that, by becoming rich, they are helping their country. To prove it they may display a symbol of staggering banality which appears to been left over from some 1950s reject sale.

The scheme has been going since 1965 and there is no record of anyone being motivated to do something they might not have done – just as well, as pursuit of profits is probably a shrewder course – but it keeps civil servants in employment.

Quotas

Foreign goods can be kept out by a general ban or the exclusion of specified items, by imposing tariffs or duties to make some goods too expensive, by devious means like enervating bureaucracy and testing procedures, or by setting a ceiling on the quantity permitted in. The ceiling, often to protect domestic makers or the currency, is called the quota. It is understandably unpopular with exporting countries which try to negotiate about removal of quotas, and threatened retaliation. The World Trade Organization (qv) is also against them and spends much of its time trying to reduce quotas.

Queen's Award for Industry

Quotation

Another word for listing, which is more usual in the US and means being traded on the Stock Exchange. Getting there is tortuous since there are the complex requirements of the Companies Act, plus the Stock Exchange's own rules about how the company can get a quote (there are seven ways of bringing a company to the market), what information it must provide and how it must behave in future.

R

Ramp

A shady operation usually operated by a group to inflate a share price, usually in the hope of selling their holdings quickly before the price drops back again.

Random walk

The theory that future share prices are impossible to predict because the direction and size of movement results from random variations that not even statistical analysis will show to be patterned and is therefore the opposite of chartism (qv).

Ratios

See Current ratio, Dividend cover, P/E ratio, Yield.

Real

Reality is just an illusion, especially in finance. Often figures are called real (real wages, real earnings, real rate of interest etc) and sometimes they are called true. All it means is that some of the distortions have been removed.

Real wages, for instance, remove the inflationary element. So if pay rises 10 per cent but inflation has been 6 per cent, the purchasing power or true wage has risen 4 per cent – more or less, since not everyone suffers to the same extent from average price rises as measured by the Retail Price Index. Unions, however, tend to insist on staying ahead of inflation and thus cause it: the snake devouring its own tail.

Similarly, real production is the value of output minus the inflationary element. This usually done by the index for that commodity.

Real rates of interest can, however, mean either the cost above the rate of inflation or adjusting repayments to cumulate the true interest rate (see True rate of interest).

There is also real property. This is a semi-legal concept referring to freehold land, to differentiate it from personal property like chattels. Hence the US term for land and buildings is real estate and the person who deals in them, the US version of the estate agent, is the realtor.

Real time sounds an odd idea, prompting metaphysical and science-fiction thoughts of unreal or notional time. In fact it is the prosaic computer term for calculations immediately on data being fed in, as contrasted with batch processing overnight.

Receiver

If a company is slipping ever deeper into the financial mire there comes a time when its creditors decide that enough is enough, and intervene to ensure that there is money to pay existing debts, let alone the ones still being piled up. In other words, they have lost faith in the ability of existing management to prevent an existing crisis deteriorating to financial disaster. They then appoint a receiver, usually a senior accountant, to act as manager and so rescue the company through tougher financial controls, or at least to keep it running long enough for cash to be squeezed out of the assets. Receivers are appointed by secured creditors such as debenture holders, or (most commonly) by banks. Courts can also appoint receivers in complicated sets of circumstances. Sometimes the receiver manages to put the business back on its feet, but that is rare. More usually, they recover cash for the secured creditors and hand back the scraps to the directors. If, as is often the case, these remnants are in no fit state to continue trading, the remaining creditors can appoint a liquidator (qv).

Recession

An economy which is not doing well might plateau out, stagnate, or be in decline, recession, depression, or slump, in order of increasing gravity. So recession is nasty but not catastrophic – unlike a slump, from which no salvation seems possible in the foreseeable future, a recession is visibly only a temporary setback. Economists invent these subtle gradations in the hope that labels will be taken for explanations but know that they are just subjective terms.

Reflation

Deflation and reflation are usually taken to refer to movements in consumer demand, as opposed to inflation (qv), stagflation (qv) and disinflation (qv), which do not.

Deflation is when an economy becomes constipated through disinclination by the consumer to spend. To reflate, the government can use monetary means such as encouraging banks to lend and borrow more money, or fiscal means like cutting VAT or income tax. One measure with a high efficiency (the money is not diverted to savings) is increasing old age pensions. More money means more demand, production increases and if manufacturers believe the upturn will continue they invest in capital equipment and hire more labour. That in turn injects more activity and cash into the economy and so leads to yet greater reflation.

Britain's manufacturing sector creaks a bit and the danger has been that added demand has led to higher prices and more imports. That has led Chancellors to damp down demand – disinflation through deflation.

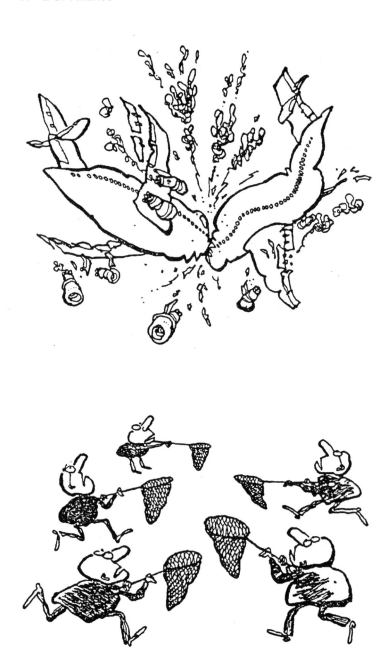

Reinsurance

Reinsurance

Insurers taking on a really big risk worry about the financial exposure. A wise precaution is to reduce the risk by insuring against having to pay up, and this reinsurance is similar to the way bookmakers lay off some of their bets. The cost will reduce profits but that is offset by the comforting knowledge of reduced chance of being ruined if say two jumbo jets collide low over Los Angeles.

The one who accepts the reinsurance can then pass it on further through what is called retrocession. By this process most big risks diffuse through major markets, and some underwriters find the risk they pushed out through the front is creeping in through the back.

Relative price effect

This is the difference between inflation in the public sector (five relevant price indices) and that in the rest of the country (measured by the gross domestic product factor cost price index – known to its friends as the gdp deflator). The public sector is permanently around 0.6 per cent higher, or some 2.5 per cent over the period of a five-year rolling plan. This is partly because pay has been rising faster than prices (improving standard of living) so the public sector's huge labour force of civil servants, health service, military and so on push up costs. But there are other reasons as well.

Relative strength

Measuring the performance of an individual share against the market as a whole (usually against the FT-SE 100 Index).

Reserve currency

Not the financial lump in the mattress but higher finance. International trade is easier if prices are set in better known and more stable currencies rather than getting involved in the Vietnamese dong, the Salvadorian colon, the Guinean sily, or the Papuan kina. So trading balances are also held in the readily convertible currencies, such as dollars, sterling, Swiss francs, Deutschmarks, yen, and special drawing rights.

Reserves

The country's financial reserves, the national current bank account, are officially known as the gold and convertible currency reserves, and are made up of gold bars, special drawing rights, credits at the International Monetary Fund, and convertible currency. They accrue not just from trade but from deposits by overseas investors which show faith in a country and its economy. But like all current accounts, the figure shows only part of the picture. Just as a person may have a deposit account and houses, so Britain has other assets including holdings at other central banks, plus property and other investments overseas.

Retail prices index (RPI)

Everybody's spending pattern is different, so the measures of inflation which deal in averages will not reflect individual experience. But some convenient measure is needed and the Department of Employment compiles a monthly estimate called the retail prices index, often referred to as the cost of living index.

The weightings are adjusted from time to time to reflect the changing average in shopping habits, but food, including soft drinks and catering, accounts for 18 per cent; clothing and shoes 6 per cent; housing including rent, mortgage etc has risen to 20 per cent; motoring is 14 per cent; and alcohol accounts for 7 per cent of the index.

From time to time the index is rebased (another point is selected for the 100 base reference level), which makes comparisons so difficult that nasty suspicions are aroused about what the government is up to. All the same, we can see roughly that what it took £1 to buy in 1998 would have taken 1.5p in 1900. To put it the other way about, what was £1 in 1900 would on average have cost £66.50 by 1998.

Retail Prices

Reverse take-over

Strictly speaking, this means no more than the reversal of normal expectations in a small company taking over a larger one. But the expression is sometimes used of the major group apparently buying a small one though the whole deal has been managed by the tiddler which is in fact about to run the amalgamated organization.

Reverse yield gap

Equities should produce a higher yield than government securities because the risk is greater. The difference is the yield gap. Occasionally, the market is perverse enough to provide higher returns on gilts and this is then measured by the reverse yield gap. The reason is the government need for cash being bad enough to outbid industry.

Comparison is generally between 2.5 per cent Consols (qv) and the FT Ordinary Index (qv).

Rights issue

Companies needing extra capital often go first to existing shareholders, and it seems fair enough that those who have already demonstrated their interest and backing should have first option to help the business to grow.

They are given the right to subscribe for extra shares in a ratio to existing holdings, usually at below the prevailing market price. If a shareholder does not want to participate they can refuse the issue or sell the new shares immediately.

Rolling targets

One way of avoiding the odium of missing aims is to have them recede and change – it is allowed to government but not to industry. Ostensibly the reason is to prevent the drastic action needed near the end of a period to achieve targets, which shows a defeatist attitude, in practice it is to stop Chancellors looking silly.

Round tripping

There is a special type of arbitrage when bank customers draw on overdraft facilities in one bank and lend at a higher rate in the interbank market, or via Paris and Amsterdam in the eurosterling market. This is a round trip. Obviously this is possible only when markets are distorted and produce a cash shortage. This is often at banks' make up day (the third Wednesday of each month when banks reconcile their books and so need the required reserve assets) but occasionally happens at other times. Apart from annoying the banks, the practice inflates money supply figures without causing actual change.

Royal Mint

The tasty job of literally making money was too valuable to be left to just anybody and has a royal prerogative in almost every country. Herodotus said there was a mint in Lydia in the 8th century BC, and the Roman occupation brought the technique to Britain. In London the mint looks to have been established about 825 and kings enforced their control by severe punishment for offences against the currency. For instance, Henry I had the hands of 96 coin makers cut off for producing substandard goods and emasculation was not uncommon. Another indication of royal control is the figure of Britannia in the 17th century, which was modelled on Frances Stewart, later Duchess of Richmond, a mistress of Charles II.

Master of the Royal Mint is the titular head of the organization, but it is a sinecure which has been held by Sir Isaac Newton and Sir John Herschel and is now part of the titles of the chancellor of the exchequer. The actual running is in the hands of the deputy master.

The actual job was transferred to Llantrisant in south Wales in 1968 but the site where the works were established early in 1811 opposite the Tower of London is still referred to as the Royal Mint.

One of the traditions is for monarchs to face in alternate directions, but this was broken by Edward VIII, who from vanity because he thought it showed him to advantage or sentimentality (accounts vary) insisted on facing left as his father George V had done.

SAEF

The SEAQ automatic execution facility – the Stock Exchange's method allowing brokers to buy and sell small parcels of shares automatically through the computerized prices display system. They just press a few buttons and the trade is done, though larger orders will still have to be agreed with market-makers over the telephone.

Say's Law

Put forward in 1803 by French economist Jean Baptiste Say, the law says production creates its own demand. Frequently misunderstood or wilfully misused as a club to beat publicity and marketing, it is actually a simplistic statement of economic equilibrium. People are paid for what they produce, explained Say, so the totality of incomes must equal the totality of production value. Increasing production therefore puts up incomes, which will generate demand for the goods. Clearly this ignores savings, overseas trade and government imbalances, and is now seldom taken seriously.

Scorched earth

Some companies will do almost anything to avoid being taken over, to the very edge of suicide. These defensive measures have reached their extreme in the United States, where the scorched earth policy was invented. This involves selling off all the most valuable assets which were what attracted the predator in the first place.

Scrip issue

An apparently unwonted burst of generosity sometimes prompts companies into issuing extra shares to existing holders at no extra charge. It is not pure philanthropy – the issue is little more than window dressing or a book-keeping exercise. As a company ploughs back profits and increases its reserves it gets steadily rising income and the dividend percentage begins to look embarrassingly high. Dividends of 60 per cent could prompt political mutterings about greedy capitalists, although a rising share price would have offset that so the yield on investments would still be in line with the market.

That is another reason: for some obscure reason British investors are nervous of highly priced shares, so a one-for-one scrip issue (one new share for each one already held) would halve the price and increase marketability. The Trustee Investment Act 1961 requires of investments a minimum share capital of £1 million, so some companies can also be promoted into trustee status. It is just a smokescreen. For the company it merely capitalizes the reserves (which is why the proper name for it is capitalization issue) and so just transfers the money from one line of the accounts to another. Transferring a sum from reserves to issued share capital makes not a scrap of difference to the company, and as the share price adjusts the shareholders are also unaffected.

Scripophily

One really would not believe such preposterous words would catch on but this 1970s term seems to have stuck. It describes the collector of shares not for the Stock Exchange value but for their pretty looks. Much sought after are 19th-century Brazilian, Chinese, or imperial Russian and the like, because they have such splendid engravings of steam trains, factories and urban scenes. So much so that when the Russians offered a niggardly 10 per cent or so redemption value (totally ignoring 70 years of unpaid interest) in 1987 many people said the antique value or the looks for lampshades or framing, seemed preferable.

SEAQ

Stock Exchange Automated Quotations system, which is a computer-based trading scheme that displays the market-makers' buying and selling prices in the offices of brokers and a few of the larger financial institutions. Small orders can be dealt with automatically. The computer is also a safeguard for investors because it registers the size, time and price of every deal and so ensures that deals are executed at best available prices.

Seasonal adjustments

There are lies, damned lies, statistics, and seasonally adjusted figures. Several government statistics are issued as straight figures and also adjusted by a smoothing factor which purports to remove regular seasonal variations and so show whether the change is real or merely reflects normal movement for that time of year. Sometimes only adjusted figures are published, which makes one suspicious, and on occasions they provide only seasonally adjusted index numbers, and then heaven and a few government statisticians only know what the figures mean.

Adjustments add almost as much confusion as they remove. Take housing, for example: building activity slows during winter because snow and ice make construction difficult, but picks up sharply during the first warm weeks of spring. But what of winters when the weather is milder than some Junes we have had? Or of winters that arrived at the start of March? And how spread out or even is the recovery period, and does it depend on the length or severity of the winter? In addition, market circumstances and labour conditions change so representative years get more elusive. The Central Statistical Office beavers away so earnestly to make the figures mean something that it seems almost churlish to complain that one is being confused – and sometimes rendered incredulous.

Secured

One of the safer sorts of paper issued by companies because, unlike ordinary shares, it is a loan against which some asset is charged, so the lender in fact holds a mortgage. A floating charge attaches to debtors or fluctuating items like stocks and does not become fixed until liquidation. Unsecured notes or loan stock are acknowledgements of debt, or promissory notes, without specific assets charged against the sum. So the investor has only a general claim against the company. When a company goes under, secured creditors are likely to be paid something but unsecured notes are further down the line for payment and there is small chance of getting their money back.

Securities and Exchange Commission

The US watchdog body supervising investment markets. Its disclosure requirements are far more extensive than anything in Britain but the resulting enormous piles of incomprehensible paperwork plus its portentous and bureaucratic methods have been the principal reason why the UK has opted for practitioner regulation (ie the markets regulate themselves), despite the obvious dangers.

The Securities and Futures Association

One of the regulatory organizations set up under the Financial Services Act 1986, and intended to keep a watch on Stock Exchange members and their dealings until it became part of the Financial Services Authority.

Securities and Investments Board

The main body set up by the Financial Services Act 1986 to supervise investor protection. It was superseded by the Financial Services Authority.

Securitisation

If one has lent someone money, all one has is a surety (or IOU, or whatever) until it is repaid. But one may need cash as well, in which case it would be nice to pass on the debt by selling it to someone else. When banks do this with, for example, mortgages, they convert the financial business in the banking system to the capital markets by issuing a series of securities against the original loan. It was much accelerated in 1985 when western banks found themselves with irrecoverable Third World debts.

Self-regulatory organizations

Set a thief to catch a thief has always been a popular notion and on the assumption that City professionals will be more expert on the dodges than any public official, the Financial Services Act delegated supervision to people within the industry. An alternative analogy might be poachers turned gamekeepers. But all the same, the Securities and Investments Board is supposed to keep an eye on them.

Senior debt

Not necessarily older, just better established. This is the first tier of corporate debt, often raised from banks, secured against solid tangible assets. If the business falls over these lenders' money is still safe.

Serious Frauds Office

Not a counterpart to the frivolous frauds section but the 1987 creation of a specialist squad to pursue the large-scale fraudsters who were assumed to bewilder the normal legal and police minds in the Fraud Squads and the Director of Public

Prosecutions' office. The parallel assumption that those sophisticated crooks would be unable to baffle the specialists has not been supported by subsequent evidence.

SETS

That should actually be SEETS, because it stands for Stock Exchange electronic trading service, but perhaps that sounded too much as if the market were resting. It is the latest phase of the London exchange's revamping. The exchange has a long tradition of producing elaborate proofs that its system is the best in the world and then abandoning it to emulate practice elsewhere.

The Stock Exchange Electronic Service in 1997 eliminated the middleman, once called the jobber and then renamed the market-maker, with a computer. Orders to buy or sell shares are fed into a computer which matches the opposing parts of the deal. However, the market failed to go the whole logical way by getting rid of the stockbrokers as well. So the broker still presses the computer keys as required by a customer to enter into the computer the buy or sell order and the accompanying criteria.

That entry process starts at 8 am but the computer does not start matching buy and sell orders until 8.30 and stops at 4.30 pm. There are four types of orders: limit (eg buy at up 130p a share); at best; fill or kill (all or nothing – complete the whole deal as specified or stay away); execute and eliminate (do as much as one can at the specified price).

This was a response to threats by Tradepoint's electronic trading system. It follows at a respectable distance the automated order book introduced in Toronto in 1977, and Paris in 1986. The system is restricted to FT-SE 100 shares, the reserves ready to move in and the former members. That is because such a trading mechanism works well only on liquid stock with lots of two-way trading, the rest will continue to work on the quote system

The theory was that this should reduce costs by taking out the jobber's turn and so the spread between buying and selling prices was expected to fall to 0.2 per cent. In fact it can make trading dearer because the system throws up some pretty erratic prices at the start and close of trading, which made traders wary of dealing early.

Settlement

Payment for shares bought has to be within five days of the deal and that is taken as the settlement time.

Share premium

When a company floats it can generally sell its shares for a substantially higher price than their face value. This difference between, say, the 20p nominal value and the 60p sale price is the share premium and companies show it in the balance sheet under the share premium account. It is hard to know why they bother, since the money is still just part of the share capital.

Shares

Shares are just what they say: anyone who owns them owns a portion of the company. Shareholders have not lent, they own the business. That means they are entitled to receive the company's accounts, attend its general meetings and vote on proposals. Unfortunately, too few investors exercise these rights, including the right to sack directors.

Shark repellent

Yet another means of deterring a would-be buyer of a company (see also Greenmail, Scorched earth, Poison pill). It normally involves amending the memorandum and articles of association to make acquisition harder by some devious tactic such as changing the number of votes needed to push through the purchase or by merging with another group to create a monopoly problem if the bid went through, or creating such a fleet of 24 carat parachutes (see Golden parachutes) that acquisition would be prohibitively expensive, or making the changes of director harder.

Shell company

Absolutely nothing to do with the giant oil business. This is the term for a business that is nothing but a name and a stock exchange quotation. Quite a number of plantation companies turned into shells as their estates were sold, lost or expropriated. The value lies in the ability to inject business into the empty shell without having to go through the long, expensive and tedious business of setting up a new company and applying for a listing.

Shogun

Bonds issued in Japan by overseas companies and not denominated in Yen (see also Bulldog).

Short position

An uncomfortable position: having sold more securities, commodities and so on than one owns (see Bear raid, Bear squeeze, Short sale).

Short sale

Being short of stock, commodities, currencies and the like means, as one would expect, that one does not have enough – in this context because one has sold more than one actually owns. A dodgy procedure traders indulge in when they expect the price will fall (ie they have a bearish view). That way, they can pick up the assets before they have to deliver, at a lower price and make a profit on the difference. Clearly, if they get it wrong and the price rises, they stand to lose a packet. That can be aggravated by the resultant further rise in price as the bears start buying to cover their commitments (see Bear raid, Bear squeeze).

Slump

A disastrous economic downturn with high unemployment, low business profits, falling production and decreasing consumption are the symptoms of a slump. It is worse and longer lasting than a recession.

In the true sense of the word it has not been seen since the late 1920s and early 1930s, partly as a result of the analysis and advice of Lord Keynes and partly as a result of lessons learnt by governments producing greater international co-operation to fend off the worst effects.

Slumpflation

As events produce ever novel behaviour, economists scuttle along behind hoping that a new label will be seen as an explanation. So we have slumpflation, stagflation and so on to describe events they had considered impossible, as booms were said to cause inflation and declines were accompanied by disinflation. Over the years Britain disproved this by combining falling rates of output and rising unemployment with higher inflation.

Smithsonian agreement

In December 1971 the muddle in world currencies was resolved by a series of realignments to produce a new set of parities. It was a laudable attempt at international co-operation yet within a year the system was dead. First to spoil it was Britain floating sterling in 1972, soon followed by others as countries grew disinclined to accept the discipline (or strait-jacket) of fixed parities.

Special drawing rights

After World War II three assets were used to fund international trade and settlement between countries: gold, the dollar and sterling. Gold is limited in supply, and the pound grew less dependable, so reserves and trade could grow only by allowing the US to run deficits – they grew by $60 000 million in 25 years. It could not last. So in 1969 a new currency was invented by the International Monetary Fund with value fixed at the nice round figure of 0.888671 grams of gold. Later it was redefined in terms of other currencies. The special part is to differentiate the scheme from ordinary IMF drawing rights available to all members.

Spot rate

The exchange rate of a currency or price of a commodity for immediate payment and delivery (in currencies it is in practice two days). The alternative is forward dealing (qv) for future delivery. The two prices will vary according to how traders see values moving over that period and also on prevailing interest rates.

Spread

The buying and selling prices of shares and unit trust units differ, sometimes by substantial amounts. For shares the difference, called the spread, reflects the costs and risks of the market-maker and will widen for volatile markets and infrequently traded shares, as both make traders nervous.

In unit trusts the offer price (at which managers sell to the public) includes initial management charges, while the bid price (at which managers repurchase units) is calculated by dividing the value of the fund by the number of units minus the cost of selling shares. So the spread can be 5 per cent or more.

The word can also be used to describe the diversity of investments in a portfolio. A good spread reduces the risk from one investment turning sour, which explains the popularity of unit trusts and the function of investment trusts.

Stag

Capel Court, round the back of the Stock Exchange, was called Stag Alley during the 19th century. That was the time of railway mania and down that narrow street prospered the Alley Men, who were sharp enough to be first in line for allotment letters for shares in the new railway companies. They then hurried down the street and cashed in on their good fortune by selling the allotment without ever having had to pay for their shares.

The stag nowadays is a similar speculator who subscribes for new issues only to make a quick profit as soon as dealings start and the price rises above the issue level. The price of new issues is usually set low to ensure they are oversubscribed (it makes life easier for underwriters) and ballots or other apportionment devices are needed, which stokes up demand. Getting extra benefit by sending in several applications was declared illegal and some people were prosecuted during the major privatization issues.

Stale bull

A more esoteric inhabitant of the farmyard in the Stock Exchange, this is the upward equivalent of a bear squeeze (qv). A bull (who thinks the market will rise) buys shares in the hope that by the time shares are delivered the price will have increased and they will then be able to sell at an immediate profit.

Nice in theory but if lots of people have taken a similar view then when the price is higher they are sitting on attractive paper profits but with nobody prepared to buy. They are then bulls going expensively stale.

Standing order

An instruction to the bank to pay a regular specified amount on a series of agreed dates, such as for mortgage or council tax. This is in contrast to direct debits (qv) when the recipient decides how much is to be extracted and when.

Stocks and shares

An investor puts money into a company in return for a receipt and a rate of return. But the range of paper issued is wide. In common usage stocks and shares are used interchangeably but stocks are in fact usually quoted per £100 nominal value – though fractions are sometimes dealt in – and examples are government stocks, corporation stocks, debentures and so on. Companies issue shares with a nominal or par value (eg 5p, 10p or 25p) on which dividend is paid when the company can afford it. Unlike stocks, they are not divisible.

Stock Exchange Automated Quotations

See SEAQ.

Stock Exchange Electronic Trading Service

See SETS.

Stock index futures

One of the increasing range of financial futures contracts which allow one to gamble in just about everything to do with money. This one is a bet on how the Stock Exchange Index will move.

Straddle

It sounds uncomfortable but in the options market it is a relatively safe gamble: it consists of buying a 'put' and a 'call' option in the same stock at the same exercise price for the same expiry date. In other words, for two small fees one gets the right both to buy and to sell a share at the price fixed on the day the deal was done. It sounds like backing all the horses in a race and so impossible to make a profit, but if the share price moves fairly sharply from the one at which the option was bought, there is money to be made: the wrong option is allowed to lapse and the other one exercised and the share immediately sold at a profit.

Structural unemployment

When industrial techniques change in a major way or when industries decline, some skills are no longer required. Farriers were displaced by cars, fletchers by guns, and Clyde-side shipbuilders were put out of work by declining world demand. The redundancies are longer term because the workers need retraining before they find new jobs. This is unemployment caused by changing structure and is separated from frictional unemployment due to inefficiencies in the system. Unions often battle against the innovations and governments are frequently under pressure to intervene. Restricting imports or taxing new products puts up prices (though allowing a longer adjustment), and propping up declining businesses deprives the new ones of cash and markets. But cars, machine tools and shipbuilding have all received taxpayer money.

Alternatively, the state can help with retraining and, since labour mobility is low, induce companies into the areas of high unemployment.

Supply side economics

Keynesian economists tend to be preoccupied with managing demand, and the reaction to that established approach produced monetarism and a school of economists with a greater interest in the supply half of the equation. One theory arising from this approach is that cutting taxes in some undefined sense releases vigour in manufacturing industry, which thereby becomes efficient and produces an economic renaissance. David Stockman, a US Budget Director, said it was what earlier economists had called the horse-and-sparrow theory: if one feeds the horse enough oats, some will pass through to the road for the sparrows. J K Galbraith, the trenchant US economist, in 1981 discouraged the American Heritage Dictionary from including the term as 'by the time the new edition comes out no one would want to know'. It was not the first time he was wrong.

Supporting a currency

When a government's economic policies produce alarm in the rest of the world, sensible industrialists start avoiding that country's currency. They assume that sooner or later disaster will strike and the currency will be worth less and by selling it their forecast becomes self-fulfilling. If the country in question feels the problems are temporary or the gloom is overdone it will try jacking up the value of the currency. The real long-term solution is obviously to remove the policies which caused alarm in the first place, and in the absence of sensible action temporary palliation can be achieved. This is normally by the central bank (in the UK the Bank of England) buying the currency, often with help from other friendly countries, but as Canute proved one cannot long resist reality.

Supporting a currency

Swap

There are many things one can swap besides stamps. Since
most financial instruments become negotiable, they can be
swapped as well. For instance, companies can raise money in
their home countries where they are known but may have
problems overseas where they want to spend. So a corporation
with low-cost access, say, to Dutch guilders but with a need for

US dollars does a deal to swap with another that has the reverse problem. Each borrows where it is cheapest and then gets the currency it really wants by a swap. This applies also to companies that have access only to variable rate loans but want fixed rate or vice versa. Clearing and merchant banks have developed and backed such schemes. It works in a similar way within a country. A company that has raised capital at a fixed rate of interest decides it would prefer to pay a fluctuating interest in line with the prevailing market rate. It then does a swap with an organization that has a reverse preference and each pays interest on the other's capital.

This leads to obvious chances for speculation in the interest rate market, in much the same way as people gamble on the level of the stock market. So, for instance, if one raises fixed-rate cash but then swaps to receive floating-rate interest one has in effect put one's shirt on rising interest rates. If one does, there is an opportunity for fixing the benefit by reversing the swap: exchanging the new high floating rate for a new fixed rate (since the new fixed rate will have to be above the cost of the original capital, there is a permanent profit on the cash). It gets more complicated with spread trading – a double swap – and even more so when companies act as go-between or market-maker because they then have to protect against risk by doing their own swaps. Not a market for amateurs. Little wonder that local authorities burnt their fingers in a market needing shrewd assessment and nimble footwork.

Swap arrangements

The reserves of a country consist of gold and other countries' currency, so by swapping currencies, two countries can increase their reserves and so strengthen the backing for their own currencies. The scheme was invented to prevent speculators knocking over a currency that was temporarily weak, partly through inadequate reserves, but not right for devaluation. Other central banks with which it has these arrangements transfer enough money to allow it to buy its own currency lavishly enough to exhaust the resources of speculators. When dealers have spent all their cash selling the currency short and find they need the money to finance transactions, they have to buy it back and the ebb has been stemmed. The central bank can even make a profit on the deal.

Britain has arrangements with 12 other industrialized countries.

Syndicate

A group of individuals who pool resources for joint commercial action. For instance, syndicates at Lloyd's (qv) have many people backing risks because the insurance requires large amounts of capital. Similarly, several banks and financial institutions may be needed to finance some of the larger share of corporate dealings.

Take-over Panel

During the 1950s a series of vicious take-overs produced some pretty shady activities, including secret negotiations and collusion between directors. This prompted sufficient concern that the Bank of England produced in 1959 a code of permissible conduct. But it became clear that, as acquisitions accelerated, a more permanent scrutiny would be needed and in 1968 a working party created the City Panel on Take-Overs and Mergers, which is its official name.

A classic piece of non-governmental regulation, the Panel has representatives from its backers in the City (Stock Exchange, pension funds, insurance companies, investment trusts, merchant banks etc) and administers the City Code. It adjudicates in take-over disputes and calls companies into line if they have broken the Code. Having no legal power the only sanction the Panel can impose is that its City supporters will shun the offender. Such ostracism denies a share quote as well as banking and stockbroking services, which few can do without and so far there has been only one case of flagrant disobedience. It has occasionally been slow or supine, but generally the Panel's virtue is the ability to adapt swiftly and to insist on the spirit rather than legalistic letter of the Code. Its purpose is to ensure open dealing and a fair treatment for all shareholders.

Its flexible power has been somewhat undermined by the European Commission's insistence on intervening as the supreme such body.

Tap stocks

Gilt-edged securities sometimes sell out on the day of issue, but sometimes a portion is held back to be trickled out over subsequent weeks via the government broker in response to market demand for stocks or to control market prices, liquidity and interest rates. These stocks are permanently on tap and hence are called tap stocks. Normally, the price is slightly lower than for other gilts of comparable redemption dates. At any time there are usually two tap stocks – a long tap with redemption about 15 years off and a short tap with maturity under five years. As one tap runs out it is generally replaced by another.

Tax

In the UK, systematic taxation dates back to Ethelred the Unready in 991. The precursor of income tax was the mediaeval scutage of knights owing service to their lords, but with a cash alternative allowed to hire a mercenary stand-in. It has seldom been well received. In 1294 Edward I's demand of half the church revenue caused the Dean of St Paul's to drop dead on the spot. An attempt in 1489 to impose a 10 per cent income tax provoked riots in the north of England. Henry VIII introduced 'progressive' tax (the rate rising with income) but that lapsed under Charles I. Pitt revived income tax at 10 per cent in 1798 and let it lapse four years later – but only for one year.

Telephone banking

First Direct awoke the public to the inconvenience of bank branches: restricted hours, long queues and a special journey. Members were allowed to carry out all transactions over the telephone at their convenience. The effect of its success has been to make its founder rich and to allow other banks to set up similar operations and close large numbers of branches.

There are still some highly suspect areas: transactions are electronic and electricity travels at the speed of light yet there is a three-day gap between the money leaving your account and being added to the recipient such as a credit card company or the electricity supplier.

Terminal bonus

A sum of money added to a policy if you reach the terminus at the end of the agreed period.

Terms of trade

An indicator of how hard a country has to work for its foreign exchange: the comparison of imports and exports by price. So if the price of imports rises faster than the price of exports, the terms of trade are becoming less favourable – ie the country has to work harder and make more goods to buy the same amount of foreign produce. In the UK the indicator is calculated by dividing the index of export prices by the index of import prices and multiplying by 100.

Thin market

A stock market term for shares that are rarely traded. They are as a result liable to move with a sharp jump of surprise when a trade does get registered.

Tips and taps

Buying shares is a bit like backing horses. One picks a runner on form, bearing in mind the state of the course (the economy), and paying special attention to the trainer and jockey (chairman and managing director). The stock market dislikes the analogy, pointing out that one rarely loses all one's money, as happens when a backed horse loses, but there is enough common language to give the game away. As on racecourses, there are tipsters in the City, but it is always worth asking why somebody should let one in on a deal, although one's participation will worsen the odds (or push up the share price), or with equal validity one may ask 'If you're so clever why aren't you rich?' A tap means someone having a large holding to be sold (has it on tap) waiting for the right price. Hence the cynical adage, 'where there is a tip there is a tap'. In other words, City people are seldom altruists.

Tombstone

An advertisement, usually taking a quarter page in a prestige journal, which looks like its name – a discreet list of names to tell the world which merchant banks have just raised large amounts of money for that client, usually by placing shares.

Tracker

Investment managers, who are so insecure about their ability to pick good stocks, or so indolent, that they make no effort at all to get a better than average return and merely track the FT-SE 100 Index. That means the obviously worrying companies in the index are included together with the solid safe performers – bear in mind Polly Peck was once in the FT-SE. So if the index rises so does the value of the portfolio, and vice versa. It requires no skill or effort but minimizes the risk of the fund manager getting it more wrong than the rest of the market.

Tracker fund

Approximately two-thirds of fund managers who pick shares to invest in with the hope of picking the real winners, do not in fact do as well as the market as a whole. So a growing number of them have opted out of trying and confessed inability by offering the ultimate of investment vehicles with no excitement and chance of being called incompetent. If you cannot out-guess the market, cannot invest any better than the average, and may well do a lot worse, the obvious answer is to buy the market. As a result, these funds track the FTSE Index (more rarely the All Share), but as buying all the shares might be a bit too much, getting into a selection that is expected to follow the performance of the whole lot.

Trade cycle

See Cycle.

Traded options

One can buy the right trade in a share at some future time at a price agreed today (see Options). A 'call' option provides the right to buy those shares at today's price so that if the price rises in the interim, exercising the option and immediately sell-ing will produce a profit. And, of course, similarly, the other way with a 'put' option. But instead of waiting for the exercise date one can also sell the unexpired portion of the option. The price will depend on the striking price (at which the option entitles one to trade) compared with the actual and expected price of the underlying security, and the period left to run. The market is always trying to ensure there are options on either side of the current market price of the share. A share at 400p will have traded options at 380p and 420p. As a result, volatile shares notch up many options as they fluctuate, though most of them have little value.

Conventional options cover three months, but traded options have expiry dates of three, six and nine months. These reduce with time and as each one expires a new nine-month 'class' is created. Normally, options trade in parcels of 1 000 shares unless they are enormously expensive. It tends to be a gambler's market but neither London nor the European Options Exchange in Amsterdam has produced the fervour generated in the US.

Trades Union Congress (TUC)

Starting from talks in 1864 the TUC was founded in Manchester four years later. It is the central organization for the majority of British trades unions, with membership of some 74 unions covering 6.7 million of the total 30 million working population.

The membership declined throughout the 1980s – according to socialists because of unemployment, according to conservatives though disenchantment with union policies. A similar decline in union membership has also been in progress in the US.

Treasury Bill

Not a man called William who runs the economy. Treasury Bills are one of the ways governments raise short-term cash. Each week up to £300 million-worth are offered for sale by tender.

The Treasury repays each Bill at par of £100 three months from the time of issue, so the discount houses and banks which bid for them pitch offers to cover the expected rate of effective interest in the money market over that period. If the tender is at £98, the rate of interest is roughly 8 per cent a year.

Anyone may tender through a bank for at least £5 000. The Bank of England runs its finger down the list of tenders until it reaches the lowest acceptable bid or runs out of Bills. So the interest rate on them reflects and influences the money market rates, and factors include the government borrowing requirement, industrial borrowing (demand for cash), flows of international money through London, and government intervention in the value of sterling.

Treasury bonds

The US equivalent of the British gilt-edged security (qv), or government bond.

Treaty of Rome

This was the document that in 1957 was signed by Belgium, France, West Germany, Holland, Italy and Luxembourg to set up the European Economic Community. It followed the 1951 Treaty of Paris creation of the European Coal and Steel Community, which succeeded in producing co-ordinated action among the six members to abolish trade barriers for coal and steel and so increasing production and prosperity. An overt aim of the Treaty of Rome is not just economic but political integration.

Trillion

See Billion.

Triple A bond

See AAA.

True rate of interest

Assessing the real rate of interest has caused prolonged anguish and argument. In the UK it is defined by the Consumer Credit Act as the annual rate of interest $100\left\{1+\left(\frac{total\ charge\ for\ credit}{amount\ of\ credit}\right)^{\frac{1}{t}}-1\right\}\%$ where t = time in years between receiving the advance and repaying the loan.

Uberrimae fides

Latin for the utmost good faith, and the basis for insurance contracts. In other contracts, the buyer is supposed to ask the right questions to find out what they is getting (though this has been modified over the years – see Caveat emptor), but in insurance it is the duty of the insured buying a policy to tell the underwriter everything relevant that may affect their insurability.

Underwriting

Another word with two City meanings: one is the financier who smoothes the way for new issues of shares, and the other is the organizer of insurance. The underwriter of a share issue guarantees the company (or local authority, central government etc) gets the funds it is raising whether or not the public subscribes for the new shares. A sudden fall in gilt-edged prices can ruin the chances of a local authority stock issue, and a wide range of factors can undermine the success of an equity issue.

In those cases the merchant banks who have in the past made tidy fortunes from underwriting rock-solid issues suddenly start earning their keep. They are left with shares that nobody wants, and since news of the failure will cause the price to sag, they must either hang on in the hope of eventually getting some benefit but thereby immobilizing their cash, or sell at an immediate loss. That is one reason new issues are set at such attractive prices. The other sort of underwriter sets the rate for insurance, in a company or at one of the syndicates at Lloyd's. At Lloyd's a lead underwriter is expected to set the terms and price and other underwriters follow their lead and conditions.

Unemployment

Unemployment figures are much less straightforward than at first appears and that makes international comparisons suspect. People looking for work but not claiming benefit are not counted, nor are trainees no matter how temporary their tuition. But the figures do include early retirements signing to avoid paying National Insurance stamps, though with little prospect of finding work. They also count the disabled and the unemployable and people in transit between jobs. In any case the figures are collected by local employment exchanges with variable care and precision so the margin of error is large.

Others fare little better. In one exercise, Belgium put its own unemployed at 7.3 per cent; the EEC recalculated that at 8.4 per cent; and the Organization for Economic Cooperation and Development assessed the same month's figure at 11 per cent. The US totals look high because they come from surveys which count people who claim to be looking for work, no matter how desultory the effort.

At best, trends are detectable but any absolute comparison is hazardous.

Unit of account (UA)

For its own accounting in 16 areas, the EEC uses the unit of account, though definitions are still not identical for all purposes. In effect, the UA is now the same as the European currency unit or ecu (qv) and is defined in terms of a basket of member currencies. It then floats against non-EEC currencies.

Unit trust

One way for small investors to spread their investments and so avoid being stuck with just one company's shares with the danger of disaster, is to buy unit trusts. It has the additional benefit (as with investment trusts (qv)) of having professionals in

charge of the investment policy. Unit trusts are, unlike investment trusts, not quoted companies with the market in units
being through the fund's managers. They are also (again unlike
investment trusts) open-ended funds, so if more savers give
them money they buy more shares and vice versa. The price of
a unit reflects the value of shares held by the trust, allowing for
a difference in buying and selling prices. So though the price
moves in sympathy with the market if the investment manager
is any good the trust should outpace the FT Index. Predictably,
many fail to better the market as performance tables show.
Unhappily those tables are poor predictors since success often
depends on picking the right sector – eg electronics, Japan, oil,
small companies, mining, commodities and so on. Indeed, one
theory says the best policy is to buy last year's poor performer.
Trusts are sometimes also linked to life assurance.

Unit trust

Unlisted Securities Market

See Alternative Investment Market.

Usury

For all those who have been abusing building societies, bank managers, credit cards, and hire purchase companies, here is the true definition. Usury laws were repealed in 1854 to encourage greater flow of capital to industry, but the Moneylenders Acts 1900–1927 regulated the interest that could be charged. They said that anything over 48 per cent a year is 'harsh and unconscionable' and anybody lending above that had to demonstrate the circumstances made it reasonable. It seems not to have been totally effective.

V

Valorise

Strictly, it simply means to set a value on – ad valorem duties
are on the basis of price – but it has come closer to Wilde's
cynic who knew the price of everything and the value of nothing. This is because the current sense of this type of setting
value is precisely in opposition to market price, and hence is
done by government.

Value at par

The nominal or face value of a share, say 5p, 10p, 20p, or £1.
It is almost always of academic interest only since it is unrelated to market price or asset backing. For government stocks the
par value is 100, the amount at which they will be redeemed.
In the US there are shares of no par value with the price determined only by the stock market.

Vendor placing

When a company buys another for shares but the sellers want
cash, the new shares must be sold before the deal can be com-
pleted. The sellers (vendors) have their shares 'placed' with
financial institutions by the bidding company's stockbroker and
so get their cash. In popular companies this has irritated existing shareholders who would prefer a full rights issue, to get a
share of the gravy. Rights issues are more expensive for the
issuing company and the shares are generally at a larger discount to prevailing price, but companies are driven to it
because groups of institutions and small shareholders are mak-

ing more of a fuss. Sometimes a combination is devised so the placing has a 'clawback' provision allowing existing shareholders to call for the shares instead.

Venture capital

A large number of funds raise thousands of millions of pounds each year to back unquoted companies. Pro rata, the UK has a larger venture capital sector than the US. So much so that it is spilling out all over Europe. Part of the reason for this is the weight of funds produced such fierce competition among the funds in the UK, that the price of investments was driven up and as a result the expected returns were coming down to quite reasonable levels. The pressure has also led venture capitalists into more innovative approaches, including buying companies for themselves, or sponsoring management teams of their own collecting.

The funds prefer large investments because they are as easy to administer as a small one, but there are fewer of them, and because large businesses have greater stability than fledgling ones. They prefer buy-outs because there is an established record of business, which makes the investment less risky than starting something new.

Venture capital trusts

Invented by Kenneth Clarke in his 1994 budget as a way of encouraging investment in small and medium-sized businesses. Quoted companies invest in unquoted securities.

Volatility

Investors looking for a quick trading profit want shares that bounce up and down by huge amounts so they can buy cheap and sell dear; long-term investors by contrast require a good steady appreciation over the years. Short-term investors can pick their potential targets by their volatility. The most common measure is the Beta coefficient (qv), which usually rates the company's shares against the market as a whole.

Voluntary restraint

This resembles army ways of getting volunteers: I want three volunteers, you, you and you. So voluntary restraint has meant voluntarily holding back pay demands, price rises, profit margins etc or being hit over the head by government. It has seldom worked.

Wage control

See Incomes policy.

Wage drift

National pay agreements followed by special local deals cause a drift away from norms for pay rises. Most visible at times of attempted restraint.

Wall Street

The New York Stock Exchange is on the corner of Wall Street and Broad Street and so the whole financial sector by extension has taken on the label in the way City describes the London financial establishment. The exchange itself is also called the Big Board and although there are many other stock markets in the US it may account for some 85 per cent of the business.

Warrant

In normal usage, a sort of guarantee, but in the stock market it is a piece of paper entitling one to buy a specified company's shares at a fixed price. These equivalents of share options can therefore be traded.

White knight

Such a romantic place, the City. An embattled company trying to fight off a take-over bid from a gritty corporate raider who will wreak havoc among management and who may dismember the company, screams for help. If it doubts its ability to defend the corporate record against an immediate offer, it may seek a rescuer – a more congenial group into whose arms it can safely sink – to make a counter-bid. This gentler alternative is the white knight riding to the rescue. Shareholders are also in favour because it means two groups bidding against each other.

Window dressing

Companies like their annual accounts to look nice, even if there are temporary problems which might prompt fears about survival or board members may be about to decamp with what is left of the disappearing assets. In such cases they massage the figures, perhaps by raising short-term funds, or by off balance sheet finance, or by touches of creative accounting, which range from the questionable through the unethical to the downright illegal. At one time, banks used to enhance their accounts by altering payment and borrowing timing to meet a cash ratio.

Withholding tax

Tax levied on dividends paid outside the country and deducted at source.

World Bank

Its official name is the International Bank for Reconstruction and Development and it is one of the two survivors of the 1944 Bretton Woods Agreement (qv). The other is the International Monetary Fund. It lends for 15 to 20 years to government agencies in member countries or guarantees private loans and so channels multilateral aid from the developed world into agricultural modernization, hydro-electric schemes, port improvements, railways etc to improve conditions in poor countries.

The bank is an agency of the United Nations and has spawned the International Finance Corporation to deal with private investors and companies, and the International Development Association, which provides loans on softer terms than the bank insists on. The Development Advisory Agency provides resident experts to help development programmes.

World Trade Organization

A reincarnation of the General Agreement on Tariffs and Trade, which was looking distinctly sickly after the Uruguay Round of tariff reductions showed that the title was a misnomer, since the GATT was characterized more by squabble and strife.

Import restrictions slow international trade and so harm the whole system. But, though governments realize this applies to others, there are always extenuating circumstances in their own case. So in 1947, 23 countries signed an agreement with the laudable aim of liberalizing world trade. Later, another 50 or so joined.

The General Agreement on Tariffs and Trade and its successor aim to stop countries raising import duties and encourage them instead to cut tariffs. There are also rules against favouritism and discrimination, which are widely ignored.

The rules say that a country should not slap on a massive duty to keep out competition, though there are escape clauses for emergencies. There are recurrent grumbles at the French and the Japanese and if members get sufficiently disgruntled they can retaliate with their own tariffs.

Liberalization is taking longer than expected, partly because free trade helps the strongest, advanced and industrialized countries. Poor countries, however, are understandably reluctant to make themselves still poorer.

The deals do not, however, cover food (mainly poor countries' exports) nor quotas and non-tariff barriers are very hard to pin down.

Writer

A seller of options contracts. So every definition is the reverse of the normal buyer's meaning: the writer of a put option, for instance, incurs the potential obligation to buy those shares at that price within the stated time.

Xd, xc, xr, xa

Shortly after a company announces its dividends the shares are quoted ex-dividend. This means the old owner remains on the company's shareholder register for a while and the buyer would not therefore receive the latest dividend. It is usually abbreviated as xd. Similarly, if a company makes a scrip issue (qv) the price is quoted ex-capitalization, abbreviated to xc on the day after allotment letters are posted to shareholders. Sometimes a company offers existing shareholders the right to subscribe for more shares and again up to the time there can be a registered change of ownership the shares are offered ex-rights, or xr. When there are several such goings on, the share is sometimes marked xa, for ex-all.

Yield

One way of assessing a share is by the amount of money it returns on the invested cash. This is called the yield. The gross yield is the percentage return at a specific price. It is calculated either as dividend in pence, divided by price in pence, multiplied by 100; or the par (nominal) value of the share in pence divided by the price in pence, and then multiplied by the percentage rate of dividend. So, in the first case, a share costing 75p and paying 6p per share, yields 8 per cent; in the second a £1 share costing 95p and paying 5 per cent would yield 5.26 per cent. What this means is that if, say, Shell yields 4.5 per cent, then every £100 invested at that price brings a pre-tax income of £4.50. Sometimes yields are quoted net of tax at the standard rate. Earnings yield is the ratio of company profits (after tax and interest payments) to total equity capital. Redemption yield is the adjustment of current yield on a redeemable stock – such as gilt-edged securities – to take account of capital gains or losses on redemption at par.

Companies expected to produce high profits and growth have high prices and hence low yields on the current dividend. Conversely, high-yielders are reckoned doubtful prospects. Fixed interest stocks respond to changes in the general level of returns on cash so when interest rates rise the price of gilts falls and vice versa.

Z-account

A privileged account at the Bank of England by such as gilt-edged market-makers, discount houses and insurance companies to certify and register gilts transfers over the counter and so accelerate a process that can take the rest of us four days.

Zero coupon bond

Bonds paying no interest but issued well below par to provide a large capital gain on redemption. Popular in the US but discouraged by UK tax rules.

Zero growth

Ecologists, neo-Malthusians, econometricians with doom-laden models and a social conscience, and conservationists tell us that it is neither possible nor moral to expect continuous economic growth in the developed world. They point to the depletion of finite raw materials and fossil fuels, as well as to the increase in world population and growing disparity between the rich and poor nations. The conclusion is that we should aim for zero growth. The case has made little impact on decision-makers or politicians, who point to the 30 years or more of oil reserves, which give ample time for technological improvements: wind, solar and geothermal power. They also dispute the reliability of statistics. History tends to support them, for humankind has proved surprisingly ingenious in avoiding extinction, though admittedly less good at preventing death and suffering.

Zollverein

The earliest harbinger of the Common Market. It is the German word for customs union and the first was established in 1833 between Prussia and the then independent German states. They agreed to abolish duties among each other and erect an external tariff wall instead. A similar approach over a century later gave birth to the EU and the European Free Trade Association.